Whose Home is This?

The Joseph Rowntree Foundation has supported this project as part of its programme of research and innovative development projects, which it hopes will be of value to policy makers and practitioners. The facts presented and the views expressed in this report, however, are those of the authors and not necessarily those of the Foundation.

Whose Home is This?

Tenant participation in supported housing

Ken Simons

North Fry Research Centre

Pavilion
PUBLISHING

JR
JOSEPH
ROWNTREE
FOUNDATION

RESEARCH *INTO* PRACTICE

RESEARCH *INTO* PRACTICE

Whose Home is This?

Tenant participation in supported housing

Ken Simons

Published by:

Pavilion Publishing (Brighton) Ltd.

8 St George's Place

Brighton

East Sussex BN1 4GB

Telephone: 01273 623222

Fax: 01273 625526

Email: Pavpub@pavilion.co.uk

In association with:

The Joseph Rowntree Foundation *and*

Norah Fry Research Centre

University of Bristol

3 Priory Road

Bristol BS8 1TX

First published 1996. Reprinted 1999.

© Pavilion Publishing/Joseph Rowntree Foundation, 1997.

A Catalogue record for this book is available from the British Library.

ISBN 1 900600 56 0

10 9 8 7 6 5 4 3 2

Editor: Anna McGrail

Cover, design and typesetting: Stanford Douglas

Printing: York Publishing Services

Contents

Acknowledgements

All researchers depend heavily on the goodwill and assistance of others. This report would not have been produced but for:

- The Joseph Rowntree Foundation who generously supported the whole project. I would particularly like to thank Jackie Wilkins, the Senior Research Manager who was directly involved in the project, for her committed enthusiasm.

- Members of the project's Advisory Group who provided unstinting advice and encouragement.

- Officers of the Notting Hill Housing Trust, including Naomi Karslake, Jenny Hindmoor and Lara Oyedele who smoothed my way and provided much practical assistance.

- Advocacy in Action, and Jan Wallcraft and her colleagues, with whom working was both an enjoyable and inspiring experience.

- The support organisations which feature in this research, including both the tenants and staff whom I interviewed. Without their generous co-operation, nothing would have been possible. I can only hope I have done justice to their views.

- My colleagues at the Norah Fry Research Centre, particularly my secretary Linda Holley who shoulders the burden of ensuring that some of my more creative literary contributions are rendered intelligible.

A Note on Terminology

The individuals and organisations described in this report use a wide range of terminology. Generally, the terms adopted in this report simply reflect those used on the ground. However, for reasons explained below, some specific terms have been used in preference to others throughout the report. These are:

- **Tenants, rather than 'users', 'clients', 'residents' or 'customers'**

There have been many arguments about the most appropriate terms to use when describing the people who make use of the personal social services. All of them have awkward associations. For example, many people with disabilities would argue that they are not 'customers' because they have little or no choice of which services they use. They cannot take their 'business' elsewhere. The advantage of the term 'tenant' is that it is widely used, and simply refers to people's formal relationships with their housing providers. It also has the advantage of not emphasising differences between the people described here and the rest of the population; most people are tenants at some stage of their lives.

- **Supported housing, rather than 'special needs housing'**

Many of the people referred to in this report might need additional help, but most of their needs are far from 'special'. We all need decent housing. Indeed, 'special needs' is a term that has specifically been rejected by some of the tenants.

- **Support or assistance, rather than 'care'**

The term 'care' is thoroughly embedded in all kinds of phrases, like 'community care', 'care providers', or even 'the caring professionals'. However, again this is a term that in its everyday use has connotations which are often resented by those on the receiving end, and rejected as patronising and, in some cases, inaccurate; some 'caring' services can be downright abusive.

- **Staff, professionals or managers rather than carers**

For the reasons outlined above, the people who work in these services are referred to either as staff (front-line workers), managers, or professionals and not as 'carers'. This also has the advantage of avoiding the confusions that sometimes arise when the term 'carers' is used to cover both paid workers, and/or informal supporters like family, friends, or neighbours.

Chapter One
Background

This chapter provides the context for what follows. After a very brief introduction it sets out the aims of the report. Definitions of supported housing and tenant participation then follow, with some discussion of why tenant participation is important. Other recent work in this area is used to highlight some of the key themes in the report. Finally, the structure of the rest of the report is outlined.

Introduction

'Associations should…encourage tenant participation…[and]…should review regularly, or consult residents and referral agencies about the running of schemes.'

This statement, contained in *The Tenant's Guarantee* issued by the Housing Corporation, is pretty unambiguous. Tenants *should* have a say in the way that housing and support services are organised. This injunction to involve people applies to 'supported housing' as much as to mainstream provision. Tenant participation is not an optional extra.

However, tenant participation is nowhere near as well developed within supported housing as it is in general 'social' housing. Concern about this gap has recently led to a number of attempts to raise awareness of the complex issues involved in ensuring that potentially vulnerable people have as much say in their lives as possible, of which this report is the latest. It is based on a small research project, supported by the Joseph Rowntree Foundation, which was linked to a Tenant Participation Initiative set up by the

Notting Hill Housing Trust, a large London-based provider of both mainstream and supported housing.

Aims

This report has three aims. These are to:

- describe the Tenant Participation Initiative

- explore the issues raised by the Initiative, through interviews with tenants, staff and managers from a range of services

- discuss the implications of the Tenant Participation Initiative.

Supported housing: complexity and diversity

Despite the increase in home ownership in the UK, many people still rent low-cost housing from 'social' landlords like housing associations and local authorities. However, some people need additional assistance to live in rented housing. This support can vary from occasional visits from peripatetic staff to full-blown residential care with 24-hour staff cover.

Supported housing is targeted at a wide range of different groups, ranging from people with learning difficulties and other disabilities, right through to single homeless people or women who have been subjected to domestic violence.

Depending on the circumstances, supported housing can provide a permanent home, a temporary option, or even a refuge in a crisis.

Most supported housing is provided as a partnership arrangement between two or more organisations. It is usually possible to identify a number of distinct roles played by the various participants. These include:

● **Housing provider**

The organisation owning the property (usually bought with funding from the Housing Corporation or its Welsh equivalent, Tai Cymru). The housing provider will be responsible for maintaining the physical fabric of the building, and carrying out repairs.

● **Managing agent**

Managing agents are responsible for the day-to-day running of the property. Staff employed by the managing agent will have regular contact with tenants and will provide help to ensure that the tenancy is maintained — for example, by ensuring that the rent is paid, and/or providing cleaning services.

● **Support providers**

The support provider, usually a voluntary organisation, provides any assistance needed over and above that required to maintain the tenancy. This could range from counselling to complete 'personal care'.

There are inevitably grey areas between the roles. For example, the difference between help to maintain the tenancy and other forms of support are not always clear-cut. Since the former can be funded through housing benefit and the latter cannot, this is not just a matter of language.

Just to complicate matters, some organisations will play more than one role. For example, often the support provider is also the managing agent. In these instances, the housing provider can end up playing a relatively passive role, with little direct contact with tenants. In this context, 'tenant participation' is likely to be more about having a say in the workings of the organisation providing support than it is about influencing the landlord.

In summary, supported housing can mean many different things; the whole concept is marked by complexity and diversity. The term can be used to describe services which differ radically in their aims, their underpinning philosophy, the way they are organised, and for whom they are intended.

As Val Feld, the Director of the Equal Opportunities Commission in Wales pointed out at a conference organised by the Tenant Participation Advisory Service in Wales,* this diversity has some important implications. Firstly, issues of **equality** will become a central concern. Secondly, there will need to be equal **diversity** in decision making to accommodate all the different experiences; single models of participation will not be sufficient.

---

* The launch of *'It Seems Like Common Sense to Me': Supported housing tenants having a say*, Cardiff, 24 April 1996.

Tenant participation... or user involvement?

By implication, **tenant** participation is about people having a say in housing-related issues. However, as suggested above, the distinction between help with housing and other forms of support can be arbitrary. For example, to someone with learning difficulties living in a residential home, where most of their contact will be with support staff, the distinction between tenant participation and other forms of 'user involvement' would be pretty meaningless.

For this reason, a very broad definition of tenant participation has been adopted for this report. It would include any mechanisms which enable tenants to influence:

● **What happens in their home**

This might be anything from deciding what colour the walls will be painted, right through to helping to choose the staff who will work with them on a day-to-day basis.

● **The organisations which provide the housing and support**

Again this could include an enormous range of different forms, from having a say in the language used by the organisations, through to helping determine the future shape of services. The mechanisms to achieve these aims might range from informal contacts through to formal representation of tenants on board and management committees.

● **The wider system**

Housing and support services do not exist in a vacuum. What they do is constrained by the way the wider system is organised and in particular by the way services are

funded. Therefore, the definition of tenant participation used here would incorporate mechanisms which help tenants try to influence that wider system, including activities ranging from being involved in developing local authority community care plans, through to voting and campaigning.

Why have tenant participation?

The arguments for tenant participation boil down into four distinct types. These are that:

● **People have a right to be involved**

This is essentially a moral argument. Regardless of the impact, people should have some control over the environment in which they live. Even if tenants opt out of them, there should still be opportunities for people to participate as of right.

● **Tenant participation results in better services**

By focusing on what tenants want, the services will become more responsive, leading to better quality housing and support that more closely fits people's needs. In other words, tenant participation is about change within services.

● **Tenant participation has a positive impact on the tenants themselves**

By encouraging tenants to become more confident and assertive, tenant participation can increase their self-esteem. Tenant participation is often seen as a key component in reversing the impact of more institutional practices within services, which have served to undermine the confidence of the people who use them.

- **Tenant participation
  is a required activity**

Like it or not, tenant participation is not
an optional extra for housing and support
services.

Most organisations will happily sign up to the
idea of tenant participation. Indeed, many
professionals are enthusiastic about the idea
of involving people, so what is the problem?

To start with, while many supported housing
services accept the principle of tenant
participation, they have yet to work out
how to organise it in practice. This is in
marked contrast to many mainstream
housing services where, even if things are
not perfect, there are likely to be some well-
established ways for tenants to get involved
in the running of the service. However, the
tenant participation structures established
in many mainstream housing services do not
generally seem to be accessible to tenants
of supported housing. The reasons for this
appear to vary, but include:

- **The geographic spread
  of supported housing**

While much mainstream housing is organised
around 'estates', where it is relatively straightforward to establish and support residents'
associations, most supported housing is
dispersed throughout local communities.

- **The confusion of organisational roles**

Again, in mainstream housing, the relationship between tenant and landlord tends to
be more clear-cut and direct. As suggested
earlier, in supported housing, the varying
roles played by support organisations have
meant that there is often no clear focus for
tenant participation.

- **Issues of exclusion**

Not all mainstream tenant organisations
have been welcoming to people who live in
supported housing, particularly where the
latter are seen to be from 'stigmatised'
groups.

Similarly, while there may be plenty of goodwill from some professionals, this on its own
is not enough. There are all kinds of pressures
which run counter to the idea of involving
people. Not least among these is the difference
in power between professionals and tenants.
The former (often without realising it) hold
all the cards. Compared with tenants, they
are more likely to:

- be better educated

- be better off financially

- have had more training

- have access to information

- have had a wider range of experiences

- be more confident and assertive

- be less isolated (most professionals
  have all kinds of support mechanisms
  ranging from trade unions to their
  partners and families)

- be less dependent on assistance
  from others.

Tenant participation is therefore about
establishing a wide range of processes and
structures which force services to listen and
respond to tenants. By embedding these in
the workings of housing and support services,
they act as a counter-balance to the other
pressures on services. As Monica Keeble,
consultant to the Welsh Tenant Participation
Advisory Service (TPAS Wales), puts it:

'We believe that tenant participation in supported housing should be a priority and part of the culture and day-to-day running of schemes' (Keeble, 1996).

Key themes

There is not enough space here to summarise the considerable literature on user involvement in general, and tenant participation in particular. However, two documents have particular relevance to this report, both based on work supported by the Joseph Rowntree Foundation, and both of which highlight a number of themes which reoccur throughout this report. These publications are:

* '*It Seems Like Common Sense to Me':* Supported housing tenants having a say, by Monica Keeble, 1996

This report recounts the conclusions of an action research project into tenant participation carried out by TPAS (Wales). It contains a number of examples of good practice. However, it also highlights some of the limitations of what is currently happening in supported housing. In particular, Keeble points to the gap between the rhetoric about services and the reality. Many of the organisations made claims which suggested that the main aims of the service they offered were about *'enabling tenants to take charge of their lives'* (a number of similar phrases were used). At the same time, the replies from the same organisations also suggested that tenant participation was not their main priority; that it tended to be seen as:

'icing on the cake', to be tackled after more pressing needs have been met.

The researchers also found that many staff saw the tenants themselves as being the main barrier to developing tenant participation:

Many perceived tenants as being uninterested in having a say.

In contrast, the researchers found that most tenants were keen to be more involved. They concluded:

'...given the right support and opportunities to develop skills, together with an appropriate approach, many tenants are interested and enthusiastic.'

Other issues the report highlights include:

- the need for tenant participation to be flexible and tenant-led, and not based on models imported by professionals

- the need to invest resources in the participation process, including ensuring that both staff and tenants have access to training, or conferences and workshops

- the importance of providing accessible information to tenants

- the need to ensure tenant participation stays on the agenda.

Service User Involvement: A synthesis of findings and experience in the field of community care, by Vivien Lindow and Jenny Morris, 1995

Lindow and Morris argue that much of the debate about 'involvement' and 'empowerment' is carried 'on the terms of' those who purchase and provide services. Involvement is *assumed* to be empowering for the users of services, an assumption which often proves to be false.

The authors also point to a range of factors which make it much more difficult for people to influence what is happening around them. the include:

- **The assumptions and behaviour of support staff**

Professional assumptions about the importance of 'professional expertise', the imposed definitions of dependence and independence, 'cultural insensitivity', and the resilience of the 'medical model' approach to people's needs all serve to marginalise the views of people who use services.

- **The way services are organised**

Financial pressures and the way services are funded, organisational boundaries, entrenched practice, the lack of alternatives, the tendency to define needs solely in terms of the existing services available locally, all serve to reduce choice and make services less flexible, thereby limiting the impact that those who use them can have on services.

- **The lack of tools to make an effective contribution**

People often lack the personal support, the information, and the resources (particularly in the context of the poverty of many people who use services) to make an effective contribution within the mechanisms that do exist. The lack of these basic tools undermines the capacity of people to influence events, particularly where attempts to involve people in decision-making structures have been on the basis of 'business as usual'; in other words, where people have had to adapt to the existing structures, rather than adapting those structures to the needs of the participants.

Lindow and Morris also describe a number of issues which are common to many of the contexts where people are taking part in some kind of participation forum, including the crucial questions of:

- **Who sets the agenda?**

Who defines what a forum is about, and who controls the process? All too often people who use services are excluded from these crucial areas of decision making.

- **Who speaks for whom?**

Arguments about representation and 'representatives' crop up again and again. On the one hand, users of services who are articulate find their views being dismissed as unrepresentative by professionals who themselves have little idea what other users think. On the other hand, there are real concerns about how to ensure that the voices of the most marginalised groups are heard. There is a danger that tenant participation will be become a mechanism for boiling down the experiences of people to a nice convenient (for organisations) single 'view', as opposed to recognising the diversity of people's experiences.

Lindow and Morris also argue that genuine participation implies a willingness on the part of services to act on what the users of services tell them, a willingness which is not always apparent. Effective participation also implies fundamental shifts in relationships between those who use and those who provide services, including in some cases the development of user-led services.

The structure of this report

The remainder of this report is structured as follows:

Chapter Two provides a description of the Initiative set by the Notting Hill Housing Trust. Central to this Initiative was the involvement of two groups of 'user' consultants. Their views are included in this chapter.

The next two chapters are based on a series of research interviews. These are introduced briefly in the box below, with more details in the *Appendix*.

Chapter Three focuses on the views of the tenants. Their experiences of and attitudes towards Tenant Participation are described in some detail.

Chapter Four switches tack and explores the issues from the perspective of staff and some organisations involved in providing supported housing.

Finally, *Chapter Five* attempts to draw together the different strands of the report, and to point out the broader implications of the findings.

The research interviews

The aim of the research interviews was to explore the issues raised by the Tenant Participation Initiative with the people most directly involved. Eleven of the organisations working in partnership with the Notting Hill Housing Trust were prepared to be involved in this phase of the work. These organisations represented a broad cross-section of the services provided through the Trust's housing.

In total, contact was made with:

● **48 tenants**

The contacts with tenants took the form of either individual qualitative interviews or small group discussions. Built around a simple list of topic areas, these were designed to be as flexible and as informal as possible, allowing the researcher to adapt to the concerns of tenants, and to the very different ways in which the individuals involved communicated.

● **15 professionals**

The interviews with professionals were semi-structured, and designed to explore both the organisational view of tenant participation, and what was happening at a very local level in each house represented in the study. The interviewees varied from front-line staff to senior managers, with most having overall responsibility for one or two specific properties.

See *Appendix* for further brief details. ■

Chapter Two

The Tenant Participation and Advocacy Initiative

In 1994, the Notting Hill Housing Trust set up a special Initiative to promote tenant participation and advocacy in the supported housing they provide. As part of this Initiative, the Trust took the imaginative step of including events led both by people with learning difficulties and former users of mental health services. This chapter describes that Initiative, and also briefly provides some background information about the Notting Hill Housing Trust.

The Tenant Participation Initiative

Like many social landlords who provide both mainstream housing and supported housing, Notting Hill Housing Trust (NHHT for short) had become increasingly aware that there was wide disparity between the two groups of tenants in the extent to which they were able to have a say in the housing they used. As far as the mainstream tenancies were concerned, there were a number of established structures enabling tenants to make their views known to NHHT, including tenants' associations. Indeed, for some years there had been mainstream tenants' representatives on the Trust's Board of Management. However, few, if any, people in supported tenancies were getting involved in these established structures.

This continues to be the case. For example, in 1995 NHHT organised a conference for tenants. Although targeted mainly at the mainstream tenancies, everybody in the supported housing was invited. According

to NHHT, not a single supported tenant went to the event.

Nevertheless, back in 1994, the lack of involvement of people from supported tenancies in these mainstream structures was an issue within the Trust. As indicated in *Chapter One*, one of the reasons sometimes cited for this lack of engagement is resistance from mainstream tenants, who sometimes appear less than willing to embrace the involvement of people from stigmatised groups such as the recently homeless, or users of mental health services. In the case of NHHT, it was actually the tenant representatives within the Trust who were pressing for some kind of action. They saw their role as being to increase tenant participation, and here was a group of people who were clearly missing out. Out of these concerns arose the Notting Hill Housing Trust Tenant Participation Initiative. Implicitly, at this stage, there was an assumption that the possible outcome of the Initiative would be either the inclusion of supported tenants in the established structures, or that there would be the development of some Trust-wide mechanisms specifically for supported tenants.

However, as Naomi Karslake, the Quality Development Manager at NHHT points out, the Trust is in a complex position. As a housing provider, part of the Trust's role is to protect the rights of tenants, one of which is to have a say in their housing and support services. However, as the term 'partnership'

implies, the Trust is not in a position to dictate to the organisations with whom they work. Nor, Naomi adds, would they want to be 'too prescriptive'. The sheer diversity of the services provided by NHHT means that what works in one context might not be so appropriate in another.

The Tenant Participation and Advocacy Initiative represented a chance to raise the wider issues with all the different 'stakeholders', including the tenants themselves.

The Notting Hill Housing Trust

The Notting Hill Housing Trust is a large provider of affordable housing across London. The organisation has over 11,000 mainstream tenancies, as well as supported housing for more than 700 people who are either vulnerable or potentially vulnerable in some way.

The NHHT represents a good example of the diversity of supported housing. The Trust works with some 36 different non-profit partnership organisations. These range in size from some of the largest high-profile voluntary organisations with a national standing, right through to tiny groups who support just one house.

The supported housing is targeted at 12 distinct groupings of people:

- people with learning difficulties
- users of mental health services
- vulnerable single homeless people
- ex-drug users
- ex-alcohol users
- ex-offenders
- women and children escaping domestic violence

- refugees
- young people leaving care
- elderly people
- people with sensory impairments
- people with HIV/Aids.

Most of the housing is shared, with only about a quarter of the tenancies in self-contained flats or bedsits. The level of support varies widely from house to house, ranging from residential care (with waking night-staff), to situations where a member of staff calls just once or twice a week.

Most of the people living in NHHT's supported housing have been there a relatively short time; in 1994 only 24% had been in their current home for more than two years. That partly reflects the fact that some houses were relatively new, but it is also because a substantial proportion of NHHT's housing is temporary; there is an expectation that people will 'move on' to more permanent accommodation, although the speed with which this happens ranges from as little as three months to as long as three years. ■

There were basically three separate elements within the Initiative:

- a survey of tenants' views
- user-led consultancies
- the formation of a 'good practice' interest group.

These different elements are described below.

The survey

This was the first element of the Initiative to be put in place. It was originally conceived as a straightforward postal questionnaire for tenants. However, a pilot showed that some of the tenants would be excluded by such an approach. It was clear that some alternative was required, particularly for people with learning difficulties.

It was at this point that the group Advocacy in Action became involved. This radical group (see the box profiling the consultants on page 14 for more details) has a well-established reputation for their work both with people with learning difficulties and with professionals. They were recruited by the Trust, with a brief to make sure that the views of people with learning difficulties were included in the survey. A similar kind of role was played by Jan Wallcraft, a former user of mental health services, who was working with a loose collective of other former service users (again see the box on page 15). Jan and her colleagues were to concentrate mainly on the high-support mental health services. The remainder of the supported tenants were sent a written questionnaire.

A brief summary of the findings from the survey is included in the box overleaf.

Once NHHT had the survey report, a number of different lines of action were set in train.

These included:

- producing a summary of the issues for each agency
- feeding back to tenants via the attendance of the NHHT Tenant Participation Officer at house meetings (*'We were keen to reinforce the message that the tenants had been heard'*)
- raising issues at the annual monitoring meetings that NHHT holds with all their partnership organisations.

The consultancies

Having set the process in train, NHHT wanted both to keep the momentum and to act on the findings of the survey. Advocacy in Action, having helped with the survey, were also keen not to leave things at that; they wanted to be involved in helping the tenants in the longer term. It was out of this interest that the second stage of the Initiative was born: the consultancies led by both Advocacy in Action — who were to work with the services intended for people with learning difficulties — and Jan Wallcraft and her colleagues — who had the broader remit to work with the wide range of remaining services provided with the involvement of the Trust.

In the face of the sheer diversity of the situations in which NHHT were involved, the initial assumptions that the Initiative would lead to the development of Trust-wide structures had been more or less abandoned. By this stage there were no clear overall goals for the Initiative. Rather, the hope was that the involvement of the consultants would stimulate the development of many different levels of involvement in lots of different contexts.

Results from the Notting Hill Housing Trust survey of tenants' views

The survey posed tenants questions on a range of topics including: the quality of the physical environment; the standard and speed of repairs; safety and security; staff support; information provided to tenants; and participation. The questionnaire was completed by 246 individuals, making up 34% of all supported tenants.

On the whole, the responses to the survey were largely positive about the services provided by the Trust. For example, over 80% of the tenants considered the decor of their room, house or flat to be good or very good. However, some important criticisms did emerge. For example, half of the tenants said they had experienced some noise in their house, and that over a third had been 'disturbed' by this.

Other areas of concern included:

● **Participation**

Over a third of tenants (37%) said they were not involved at all in making decisions about their house, with a further 39% saying this only happened 'a little'. This did not necessarily mean that people were unhappy with that situation. Almost half (48%) of the tenants said they did not want to be more involved. However, this still left a very substantial minority (41%) who wanted a bigger say in how things work.

● **Security**

Some 20% of tenants did not feel 'safe and secure' in their home. Similarly, 26% felt lighting outside the premises was not adequate. These feelings of insecurity were highest amongst women tenants.

● **Levels of support**

Only just over half the tenants replying to the questionnaire (54%) were happy with the levels of support they received. Of the remainder, 17% definitely wanted more support, with 23% uncertain.

When asked about the aspects of services they liked best, the most popular was **supportive staff** (cited by 22% of tenants), followed by **location** (20%) and the **degree of privacy** offered (19%).

In contrast, the most frequently mentioned 'least favourable' aspects of services were said to be having to **share accommodation** (mentioned by 19% of tenants), **noise 'pollution'** (also 19%) and the anti-social **behaviour of other residents** (13%); all of which reflect the pressures of communal living. ■

Both sets of consultants embarked on a programme of activities which included house visits and workshops. Advocacy in Action's programme included a 'top people's' day, where they and some of the tenants with learning difficulties made presentations to an audience of staff from NHHT and its partnership organisations, along with representatives from the Department of the Environment, the Tenant Participation Advisory Service and the Housing Corporation. Jan Wallcraft and her colleagues took part in a similar conference called *Hearing the tenant's voice*.

All the events were entirely voluntary. Inevitably, the organisations providing support services acted as a filter, and some were more active in taking up places than others. Most of the events were targeted at both tenants and staff, often involving the two groups as co-participants, although the variable demands meant it was often difficult to predict where the balance would lie.

Both sets of consultants were also keen to attract people from the local management committees to their events. These management committees were a feature of many of the partnership organisations, usually consisting of combinations of professionals, people from the local community, and members and supporters of the organisation involved. Again (and anticipating **Chapter Four**) only rarely were tenants or ex-tenants part of the management committee. Potentially these management committees have considerable influence on the local schemes, yet it proved difficult to interest the committee members in the events, even when they were held over a weekend to make them more attractive to this audience.

It is now not unusual, within some community care services, for people with disabilities themselves to be providing training and consultancy, particularly around disability-awareness issues. However, this is much less common in the sorts of context described in this report. For example (again anticipating one of the findings from **Chapter Four**), few if any of the organisations participating in the research reported asking users to act as trainers. It is therefore worth spelling out just some of the reasons why this is a good idea.

Firstly, offering training and consultancy services is one way for users or former users to influence new developments. Having users as the 'experts' reverses the usual relationship between professionals and users, and as such it sends powerful messages to everybody involved. The context tells staff that here are people to be listened to and respected as

equals. For fellow users, here are role models; people like themselves standing up and being assertive.

Similarly, ensuring that there is a strong emphasis on exploring the issue of tenant participation from the perspective of people who use services is one way of preventing the views and concerns of professionals and services from dominating the discussion.

Finally, user-trainers can do things that professionals cannot. They have access to direct experiences that professionals do not have, and those experiences can be an effective basis for delivering very powerful messages.*

Take for instance, the issue of labels. One of the exercises that Advocacy in Action include in their workshops begins with the people with learning difficulties doing the training holding up a card with some of the names they have been called, and the terms used to describe them in the past, written in large letters. People from amongst the workshop participants are then asked to read out these words. Many of the words (indeed most of them) will be inherently devaluing; 'sub-normal'; 'retarded'; 'mentally handicapped'; 'spastic'; 'nigger'; 'stupid'; 'thick'; 'cripple'. The list is long. The group is then invited to discuss how they would feel if those names were applied to them (or in the case of other users of services, how they have felt when these kinds of terms have been used about them). The terms used by the services represented at the workshop are also listed and discussed. As part of this process, the many negative descriptions are literally consigned to a dustbin. For a professional acting as a trainer, it would be difficult to

---

* See also Wright, L. (1996).

deal with a subject like this in anything other than an abstract way. However, having to read these words, whilst sitting next to the very person who has been on the receiving end of them, forces participants in the workshop to confront the issues of labelling in the most direct way possible.

A profile of the consultants

Advocacy in Action

Based in Nottingham, Advocacy in Action is perhaps best described as an informal co-operative of people with and without learning difficulties. The group does a range of different activities, but is probably best known for its training, targeted at both people with disabilities and non-disabled people, for which it has won national awards.

As Advocacy in Action members cheerfully admit, they have their own way of working, and their own agenda, and they very much keep to it. A key to understanding Advocacy in Action's approach is their stress on their value base — of being 'equal people'. As Julie Gosling, one of the co-workers, puts it:

'We were not prepared to provide a 'how-to-do-it' kit. We wanted to get people to look at their values first.'

By going back to values, and then getting people to work together on the implications for services, the group hopes that participants will have the resources to develop their own solutions back in their own services.

Partly as a reflection of the importance the group attaches to values, a lot of its work focuses on the issue of language. Such issues also make a good starting point for staff and the users of services to begin to work together. As they point out:

'Organisations can never say they cannot afford to change the language they use.'

Advocacy in Action's approach is marked by three particular characteristics:

- **It is very much based on their own experiences**

Many members of the group have had very bad experiences of services for people with learning difficulties in the past. They draw heavily on those experiences, redefining them in terms of 'surviving injustice'. For example, Kevin Chettle has produced a series of brilliantly coloured pictures which vividly illustrate his experiences of life in a long-stay hospital. These drawings, along with Kevin's descriptions of the abuse he experienced as an everyday part of life in the hospital (featured as part of a Channel 4 documentary on self-advocacy called *Colour Me Loud*), are one of the various tools used by the group in their training.

These experiences also serve to highlight issues that need to be confronted and challenged within services. Again to take an example, as a black woman with learning difficulties, Heather Francis has experienced racism in services. This is now an issue for the group as a whole.

● It is about celebrating difference

Advocacy in Action believes everybody has something to contribute, and should be recognised and valued as they are, not as other people think they ought to be. As Tammie Brewster, one of the co-workers comments:

'I suppose you think I would like legs like yours. Well, it's not a tragedy to have legs like mine.'

● It is inclusive

Having experienced exclusion and segregation themselves, Advocacy in Action members are very clear that they want their work to be inclusive. In particular, in the context of tenant participation, they are very anxious that people who are not able to speak for themselves (at least not in the conventional sense) are included in the process. This means a willingness to look at the kinds of messages people who do not use speech or signing are giving:

*'It means being prepared to try and interpret behaviour. For example, trying to key into why people might be distressed...It means starting from the **logic** of their behaviour.'*

Jan Wallcraft and her colleagues

Jan Wallcraft is a former user of mental health services who has become very active in training on the issues of participation and empowerment in services. During the process of working with NHHT, Jan had drawn together a loose coalition of other 'survivors' of the mental health system, including Ros Caplin, Marva Anderson, Chris Harrison, and Israel Fraser.

Like Advocacy in Action, it is their frequently negative experience of the reality of services which inspires Jan and her colleagues, and shapes their approach. As Ros comments:

'Anger is an important stage towards empowerment.'

'Consciousness raising' — helping people articulate that anger and channelling it constructively — is an important theme in the group's work. Based on a clear 'disability equality' perspective, many of their sessions were designed to explore values underpinning tenant participation, although they also tried to make sure that there was space to explore more practical issues.

One of the objectives of the group is to try to make sure that the issue of tenant participation reflects the agenda of tenants, as well as that of professionals. They point out that many people working in services assume that the 'empowerment' of tenants will lead to increased participation rates in structures that services have set up:

'Staff get very frustrated because people are not going to the disco. People are expected to suddenly get involved and forget all their past experience.' ■

The good practice group

This is the most recent development in the whole Initiative. The group, instigated by NHHT, represents a forum for the Trust and partnership agencies to meet and discuss tenant participation issues.

The response to the group has varied. Some partnership agencies are enthusiastic and well-represented at meetings, although these tend to be those that have already been working on tenant participation issues. Other organisations have shown little interest. Indeed, NHHT reported a degree of cynicism in some quarters on the subject of tenant participation. For example, some say they have tried to implement ideas like having house meetings, which then did not work.

As a result, one of the intentions is to produce a 'good practice' manual based on some of the work going on within the Trust's schemes. Taking the example of house meetings, one of the objectives would be to try to identify the tactics that had made such meetings a success in some organisations (for example, by ensuring that tenants were able to set the agenda).

It is still early days in the life of the good practice group, and too soon to identify what impact it will have. Nevertheless, it illustrates a commitment to keeping the issue of tenant participation on the agenda, and promoting and disseminating good ideas.

The views of the consultants

As outsiders involved in the process, the views of the consultants were critical. Their opinions on both the process in which they were involved, and the kinds of tenant participation they encountered, are set out below.

The experience of the consultancies

On the whole Advocacy in Action were very happy with the way their work went:

'*It was good!*'

However, the experience was not without its drawbacks. With hindsight, they would have spread their involvement out over a longer period. The visits to London, organised so as to be as efficient as possible, were acknowledged to be 'hard work'. Organising events from a distance and involving so many different organisations proved to be more complicated than expected, and one of the officers from NHHT ended up having to take on a lot of the practical arrangements. Inevitably, practical arrangements did not always work out quite as planned. In particular, because of the routines in particular houses, people would often arrive at odd times for workshops, and would have to leave early, so the group were always having to change things. Advocacy in Action are used to having a more direct relationship with organisations, and working through a third party was a new experience.

Jan Wallcraft and her fellow consultants were also very positive about many aspects of their involvement. Some of the sessions, particularly those involving both tenants and staff, had worked very well.

Not that everything had gone smoothly. For example, unlike Advocacy in Action, Jan Wallcraft and her colleagues were working with very different services targeted at different groups of people. They felt that some staff had tended to dismiss their input as 'irrelevant' because of the consultants' background in mental health issues, rather than recognising that many of the wider issues were common to everyone. Coupled with this was a tendency for some staff to get frustrated when they were not presented with simple definitive 'answers' to what are often complex dilemmas. They also found a tendency for some staff to 'blame' the tenants for what could sometimes be a frustrating lack of progress:

'They were saying, "But you haven't met our clients, they aren't motivated". People are just expected to forget the past and sign up to someone else's agenda.'

At the same time, Jan and her colleagues had found themselves struggling to define their own role. They felt that there had been no strong message about what NHHT wanted from their involvement, leaving the exercise rather open-ended.

In addition, a couple of less experienced people dropped out, and one or two others had crises which limited their involvement at different points in the process. This raises an important point. Both sets of consultants were very 'professional' about their work. They were experienced and clearly under-stood the principles of effective training. However, they were recruited precisely because they were *not* professionals. All training or consultancy work needs to be good, whoever it is delivered by. Neither set of consultants would want to be patronised by having 'allowances' made just because they are people who have, at some stage, been service users. Yet, both groups needed a degree of support from NHHT to do their work effectively. Involving user-consultants is best seen as an exercise in partnership.

Finally, both sets of consultants found it difficult to access some groups of tenants. As noted earlier, the organisations providing support to people acted as a filter. At one level this is quite appropriate. Support staff

have a role in ensuring that users of services are informed about options, and in supporting their wish not to take part in activities, if that is what they want. However, for the consultants, the suspicion remained that the apparent failure of some groups of tenants to respond to invitations was more a reflection of the lack of interest within the organisations, rather than a result of tenants making an informed decision not to get involved.

The extent of tenant participation

Both groups of consultants reported positive examples of tenant participation encountered during their work, some of which will be reflected in the later chapters. However, they also identified many areas where much more could be done. These included:

- ensuring that tenants get involved in decision-making structures, with the support to make an effective contribution

- the lack of control people have over their money in some houses

- the need for accessible information about rights

- the need for better complaints procedures

- the chance to join wider groups like People First, or Survivors Speak Out

- the lack of opportunities to be involved in interviewing and appointing new staff

- the lack of incentives to get involved in short-stay accommodation

- the lack of budgets for tenant participation

- the lack of response to some issues raised by tenants

- the lack of a say in issues like medication or treatment

- the lack of contact between tenants and 'top people'

- the restrictions on visitors in some houses.

As well as addressing the apparent gaps in participation, Advocacy in Action had a number of developments that they would like to see happening in the future. These included:

- tenants building up skills to become trainers in their own right

- tenants to be paid for their work on tenant participation, and to have access to training and support to make it more effective

- more sharing of ideas across different houses and organisations.

Jan Wallcraft and her fellow consultants were concerned that, while tenants often had a chance to influence things at a grass-roots level, the Initiative also needed to have an impact 'higher' up:

*'What about senior levels, are
they getting the message?'*

These issues raised by the consultants were used as a basis for developing the research interviews, the findings from which form the basis of the next two chapters.

Chapter Three

Tenant Participation From the Inside: The views of tenants

If tenant participation is to be judged a success, then it must work for tenants. It is vital we learn from their experiences of tenant participation. This chapter looks at tenant participation from the perspective of tenants who were using a wide range of different support services. What emerges is a very mixed picture. For some, tenant participation was a positive, empowering experience. More found the tenant participation on offer a far from earth-shattering experience. Others were angry about the apparent indifference of the service to their views. This chapter explores these very different experiences. While the main focus of the interviews was on the mechanisms of participation, the tenants were also concerned about the nature of the support services themselves. The issues of tenant participation and the kinds of choices offered by services are inextricably linked.

To recap, this chapter is based on the views of 45 tenants, contacted through a range of support services. These 45 individuals represented a very varied range of circumstances. Some were very articulate, others expressed themselves through speech with difficulty. Some tenants were living in a permanent home, others could expect to have to move on eventually (some in a very short time). Some tenants had staff present 24 hours a day, others could only expect to see a member of staff once every few days. Anticipating **Chapter Four**, some of the services they used had clearly put some effort and thought into tenant participation, while in other services tenant participation clearly took a back seat to other concerns. In such varied contexts, it is dangerous to make sweeping generalisations. Nevertheless, some common themes did emerge, as did some

very striking differences in the extent to which people felt their views were taken into account.

Messages about choice

The interviews were focused around the issue of the way that tenant participation was organised. Yet they were also designed to be as flexible as possible, allowing the tenants to raise issues that mattered to them. Inevitably, the interviews often shifted away from the specifics of how people were (or were not) involved, towards fundamental issues about the nature of the services they were using. The chapter opens with a discussion of two areas where tenants were getting negative messages about choice. These were the way in which the services offered failed to meet the aspirations of a substantial minority of tenants in terms of **housing and support** arrangements, and the tendency of the services to keep **the wider community** at arm's length.

Options for housing and support

There is a danger with tenant participation that the main focus of activity is around changes within services, without ever questioning the basic premise on which the service is provided. Having a say in where you live is probably more important in the general order of things than helping to work out the cleaning rota. The interviews there-fore began with a general exploration of how tenants felt about the service in general, and, in particular, the extent to which the use of that service represented a positive choice on their part.

The majority did appear to be happy where they were living. This was particularly the case where people had moved out of more institutional settings:

> *'I was in a hostel, and they asked me*
> *where I wanted to go.'*

> *'It's much better than [names hostel].*
> *It was noisy, horrible. Too many people.*
> *I've learnt a lot more since I came here.'*

Often the reason people gave for preferring the less institutional services reflected the greater control they had over their lives:

> *'It [the hostel] wasn't very nice. "Where are*
> *you going?", having to be back at a certain*
> *time. Here you can go where you want.'*

> *'More free here.'*

However, there was a very substantial minority (actually 22 out of the 45, about 48%) who made it clear that, given a choice, they would opt for an alternative to the place in which they were currently living. Given the qualitative nature of the research, the precise numbers falling into this dissatisfied camp are not important. What does matter is the way in which the services did not seem to meet either the aspirations or needs of some tenants, and the apparent lack of choice facing people.

Amongst the services long-term support (in this study, mainly residential homes for people with learning difficulties or users of mental health services) a number of tenants would have preferred to live in their *own* homes. This does not necessarily reflect the quality of the service they were using; rather, the fact that communal living has real limitations.

For example, one young woman with learning difficulties contrasted the pattern of life avail-able to most people with her own experiences:

> *'You want to live with your parents, then*
> *you want to live on your own, and then you*
> *want to live with your girlfriend…*
> *You can choose any home. It's difficult for*
> *me. I want to live with my boyfriend, but*
> *I can't until I have learned to do shopping*
> *and cooking.'*

Some tenants made it clear that a residential home had not been their choice in the first place. As one tenant explained, he had really wanted to live with a friend in a flat of their own. Instead his social worker had offered him a place in a residential home:

> *'I wasn't too sure at first, then I decided it*
> *would be OK. I was virtually told to come*
> *here.'*

However, that 'OK' represented resignation rather than a positive choice. This man still wanted to live in a place of his own. Significantly, even though he thought the support staff who were working with him sympathetic, he found it difficult to raise the subject of his aspirations.

Others still harboured a wish to have their own home, even though this was an option that had not worked for them in the past:

'I used to have a flat. There were problems with the local kids. I couldn't cope then. But I'd really like to have a flat again.'

It should be added that even amongst those who expressed a clear preference for their current service, this choice often appeared to reflect their assumptions that living in your own home equated to living without assistance.

'Oh no, I think I'd rather stay here. I've seen people go out [into their own flat] and they don't last six months — they're back here. You don't get help like what we do.'

Many of these concerns were echoed by people in short-term tenancies, although with a rather different emphasis. Some tenants accepted that in a crisis a temporary home was what they needed while they sorted themselves out. Their initial reaction to the service was positive:

'You get a roof over your head, and some food.'

However, others made it clear that what they really wanted was somewhere permanent to live, and were surprised that the question about choice had even been asked:

'That's a stupid question. Of course we didn't choose to be here. I had no choice…'

This anger at the lack of alternatives was most evident in the services with the shortest tenancies, where the tenants were all too aware that any 'move-on' arrangements were themselves likely to be temporary:

'They just find you a hostel on a longer term.'

There was a sense among these tenants that the system failed fundamentally to take account of their views:

'Just because we're homeless, it don't mean we have no rights.'

'I want my independence. Going from hostel to hostel won't make you independent.'

It would be a remarkable world if everyone was happy with the choices on offer. However, the fundamental lack of choice experienced by many people gives them a powerful message that their views count for little: messages that run counter to the whole thrust of tenant participation and which risk undermining initiatives designed to promote it. If tenant participation is meant to be about change, then it needs to have an impact in the areas of people's lives that are most important to them.

Links with friends and family

People's links with the world outside services are important to them in all kinds of ways. Indeed, these links and connections were often cited as the reasons why people liked living where they were:

*'I have lived in the area since 1957...
There's plenty of buses and tubes. I've
got friends around here. My sister and
brothers visit...'*

Similarly, these links were important in the
kinds of choices people wanted:

*'I want to live in Earl's Court. My friends
are there, and I know the area.'*

Yet some services, apparently almost
unwittingly, had adopted policies that had
the effect of keeping family and friends at
arm's length. In at least one service, tenants
claimed visitors were not allowed. Being
relatively large, with a high turnover of
tenants (many of whom had a drug habit)
security had become a major issue. The
front door was permanently staffed and
locked, with a careful scrutiny of all who
entered or left the building.

However, the way that outsiders were
treated was also an issue even in much
smaller, longer-term services. The story of
one particular tenant illustrates the point:

*'I used to have my daughters visit. They
used to like coming here. I could play
with my grandson in the back garden.'*

Because of concerns about petty thefts, staff
had started to become much more security-
conscious, with what this particular tenant
felt were unfortunate consequences that
affected her experience of life in the house
in a major way:

*'They used to ask them to wait in a room.
They gradually came less often. They
were effectively discouraged from coming.
Staff wanted to know who was coming
and going.'*

Some of the tenants in registered homes
also found that it was difficult to develop
relationships with people outside the house.
This was not necessarily because staff inter-
fered directly in relationships but, by its
very nature, residential care means leading
a rather public life:

*'It's not exactly the same as your own front
door. It's not that convenient to bring people
back here. There's no privacy, and visitors
have to leave by 11.30.'*

Of course, the outside world can also be
a source of trouble. Tenants in one house
mentioned complaints from neighbours,
and in another, local kids had proved to be
a nuisance (the tenants thought staff were
not doing enough here to make the garden
secure). Nevertheless, relationships with
people outside the schemes are undoubtedly
important, and the actions of services ran the
risk of leaving people more isolated. This is
much more of an issue for people who are
in temporary accommodation and who are
seeking to re-establish themselves as part of
a community. When people do eventually
find somewhere permanent to live, their
informal networks are probably going to be
as important in enabling them to maintain
their tenancies as are formal services. Yet, it
seemed that some of the crisis services were
simply not geared to helping people develop
or maintain relationships.

Experiences of tenant participation

The rest of this chapter is concerned with
both how the tenants viewed the tenant
participation mechanisms with which they
had been involved, and the areas where they
would like to have a say, given the chance.
Since many of the tenants were most concerned with their own immediate lives, it is
organised from the 'inside' out, starting with

the kinds of participation on offer within the house, then branching out to look at the extent to which people were getting a chance to influence the support organisations.

Tenant participation at the most local level

There was considerable divergence of experience between the different kinds of services about the kinds of control the tenants had over their lives within their house. Some of these differences reflected the nature of the service. For example, a number of the low-support houses were really organised as a series of bedsits, with relatively little communal space. Although people in adjacent rooms might share a kitchen or bathroom, and there might on occasions be a communal lounge, there was little sense of people living together. At one level, this could mean that each tenant had more control over their lives:

'There are no rules, apart from what is in the tenancy agreement.'

'There's more freedom here. People don't interfere. You can do what you want.'

'You don't bother people and they don't bother you.'

In these services it was not unusual to hear caution expressed about anything that was communal. One man actually said he was glad there was no lounge because:

'Communal areas cause trouble.'

However, he did add that when tenants in the house did get together (in someone's room) such meetings were usually 'amiable'. The most stark contrast was with a couple of services that were based on a specifically

rehabilitative model; what might be called, for want of a better term, therapeutic communities, usually for people who were recovering either from substance abuse or a period of mental illness. In both cases, acceptance as part of the community was conditional on accepting particular rules. An example is given in more detail in **Chapter Four**. This chapter simply deals with how people felt about being asked to sign up to rules of behaviour that would not usually be required in housing and support services (for example, there was an expectation that tenants would come to all meetings organised by the services). On the whole, tenants accepted the situation:

'It's my choice, there was plenty of information.'

'There's a contract. It's all well and good. There's some structure… showing you can cope.'

'It's showing a commitment to the home, that you want to get on.'

The people who lived in registered residential homes had yet another set of experiences. Here there was clearly a more communal life, and often there were more staff around. Not surprisingly, this could result in some tenants feeling that they had little control over their lives:

'No, none whatsoever.'

There were also some complaints from tenants that staff were 'interfering':

'I'd like to decide things for myself.'

Even where staff had clearly tried hard to emphasise tenant participation, it did not always follow that tenants felt free from pressures to conform to what they perceived to be the professionals' views. As one man put it:

> '*It was **suggested** [his emphasis] to me, but I couldn't really refuse it.*'

Tenants could sometimes be conscious of quite subtle issues of control. For example, in one house staff had more or less decided by default to have a rota for jobs around the house. Tenants were said to have been involved because they were asked to choose which days they would be 'on'. Yet when one of the tenants was asked who decided things he was adamant it was 'staff'.

However, even in these high-support services there were examples of tenants who felt that their views were genuinely listened to and acted on:

> '*We all decide the rules. We sit down and have a meeting.*'

House meetings

Almost all the tenants said that there was some form of house meeting in the property in which they lived. In a couple of instances, these house meetings were run *by* tenants *for* tenants. Staff would only be there in the capacity of a supporter or by invitation:

> '*Staff are there to support: they don't take over.*'

In one case, the house meeting was facilitated by an independent outsider.

For the majority of tenants, however, the house meeting was still very much something that was controlled by staff:

> '*It's run by staff...Yeah, staff are always there.*'

There was some awareness that this situation was not ideal. For example, one house had compromised by have a 'pre-meeting' that only the tenants attended.

In some instances, organisations had gone out of their way to make house meetings an attractive proposition:

> '*They always have cakes, and coffee and drinks. It's good to talk to the other tenants.*'

In other instances it was clear that attendance at the house meetings was not optional:

> '*You have to go. Everybody comes.*'

This raises fundamental questions about the function of the house meetings in some services. Were they a forum for the tenants to express their views, or were they a mechanism for staff to raise issues with tenants? In some cases there appeared to be some confusion about these two quite distinct functions.

In general tenants liked house meetings:

> '*Very helpful.*'

Even where staff domination of the meeting was the norm, many of the tenants accepted the situation quite happily:

> '*I get on well with staff. You can rely on them.*'

However, there were a minority of tenants who were critical:

'Too much telling, not enough listening.'

'Residents should be in charge.'

Also, perhaps inevitably, house meetings could reflect the tensions between individual tenants:

'People are not nice to you.'

Control over staff

The actions of staff can have a big impact on the lives of tenants. In general, tenants were fairly positive about staff:

'You can trust them…'

However, things were often far from perfect:

'Some are OK, but some are not.
One or two boss you about.'

The tenant quoted above had a pretty clear idea of what he wanted from staff. High on his list were people who would 'listen', and who were 'helpful'. Having a sense of humour was also important. It is perhaps no accident that this particular tenant lived in a house where there were opportunities for tenants to have a say in the appointment of front-line staff, something that a couple of services had recently begun to try:

'Yes. I've started sitting on a panel. In June [1995] it started. I think it's reasonable to include us residents. After all, they [the staff] are going to be with us full-time.'

However, for most tenants there was little opportunity to have an input into the activities of staff. There were few mechanisms for influencing job descriptions or the appointment of new staff:

'We have no say whatsoever.'

'We would like to choose staff.'

This was particularly an issue for some of the tenants from minority ethnic groups, who were faced with all-white staff teams:

'The ethnicity of staff should reflect users. I'm a black man…[black staff] would see where I was coming from.'

'All staff are white…I mind it sometimes.'

New tenants

There also appeared to be few formal opportunities for people to help choose new tenants. The impact of other tenants on the quality of people's lives could be considerable:

'That can be a bit scary…when new people come. You don't know what they will be like.'

There were a few examples where tenants did seem to have been able to influence the process:

'The residents do interview new tenants. We have a bit of a say; they [staff] do take it into account.'

As **Chapter Four** shows, even in services where tenants had no formal input, there were situations where staff felt they had to take note of the very real fears of the tenants. Yet often there were no mechanisms for doing this openly; any opportunities for taking into account the views of tenants were entirely informal. These situations typically involved somebody with a reputation for bullying and who was known to existing tenants:

'There was one occasion. I didn't want someone to move in. I told [names staff]. He didn't move in.'

Information

Quite a number of tenants felt they were not really kept informed about what was happening, both in their particular house, and in the wider service:

'We are not really told what it is about, we just stumble into it.'

The amount of information that tenants reported receiving varied widely between and within services. Furthermore, the information that was provided was often not in a particularly accessible form:

'I didn't really understand it.'

As a result, most tenants relied on staff going through particular documents or procedures.

'[Names keyworker] would explain it.'

Perhaps because of this, important documents like tenants' handbooks appeared to be little used by tenants (if they had one in the first place).

Even where this information had been provided, the message did not always get through. For example, one tenant was overheard by a member of staff saying that he had not been told about a particular aspect of the home's policy. The member of staff pointed out that this was a subject which was dealt with at the interview when tenants first arrived. The tenant did vaguely recall this was the case, but pointed out there was a lot to take in at that interview, at a time when everything was strange and unsettling.

Budgets and money

In some of the services, the control of some budgets had been delegated to the tenants. For example:

'There is a budget for trips…We decide, with advice, about what is feasible.'

Inevitably, these delegated budgets tended to be small and vulnerable when services were under financial pressure. For example, one house had previously had a 'haircutting' budget; however, much to the disgust of one particular tenant, this was no longer available:

'We used to get razors and soap and toothpaste. But they have been cut and we have to buy them now. It was never discussed, and they didn't say why.'

Indeed, in general, services did not seem very good at accounting for their financial decisions. So, for many tenants, it was not at all clear how rent and/or service charges were decided:

'I'd like to know how they arrive at that. You don't really know what's happening, if they are in budget or making a fortune.'

The kind of service people were living in also made a difference to the extent tenants were able to exercise control over their money. So, for example, people living in unregistered settings were typically able to cash their benefits themselves, paying their contribution to rent or services charges out of this. How this is managed is more complicated where people have difficulty with money, but even here the principle that people should have as much control as possible still applied, and there were plenty of examples of people with learning difficulties cashing their own benefits and, with appropriate help, paying their own bills. However, people in registered homes were usually in a very different position. Most of the money which pays for their placement goes direct to the service in question; individual tenants often only get the standard 'personal allowance' in their hands:

'I only get £13 a week.'

Decor

While some tenants — particularly those in more permanent settings had been given a chance to choose the decoration or furnishings for the house, this was much less likely in temporary accommodation, largely because of the sheer turnover of tenants:

'The room was decorated by the previous tenant. It's OK, and I was offered the chance to redecorate it.'

Some obvious opportunities seemed to have been missed. For example, one woman explained that she had experienced difficulty sleeping, and that in the end the service had changed her bed. However, she had not been involved in choosing that replacement.

Influencing the organisation

On the whole, tenants reported relatively few experiences of involvement with support providers outside of the immediate house in which they lived. This might be partly because some of the activities involved were infrequent 'one-off' events which receded in tenants' memories, and which were recalled only after a prompt.* However, this was undoubtedly also because there

___
* This happened a couple of times in situations where staff had already mentioned some event to the researcher.

were generally few chances to engage with the organisation. Indeed many tenants, particularly those living in short-term accommodation, had little sense of the organisation behind the support services. To them, the rest of the activities of the support providers (and of the Notting Hill Housing Trust) were largely invisible. As a result, there were many areas of policy and practice which tenants felt they had little scope to influence:

'Oh it's [the rent] a bit heavy, but there's nothing I can do about it.'

Contact

'We don't see any of the bigwigs.'

As this remark above suggests, there was little evidence of senior managers having much direct contact with many tenants.

This was in marked contrast with experiences of the tenant who could name the director of the support organisation:

'Oh, it's Christian names when he comes. Very good, he creates a nice atmosphere; very approachable.'

This is certainly an issue that a number of tenants thought important. For example, when one woman with learning difficulties was asked if she would change anything if she were in charge, she unhesitatingly said:

'I would come and see everybody.'

In a couple of other instances, tenants clearly had a presence in the local 'office':

'Oh, yes, the people in the office are very nice and helpful.'

Although being able to use facilities in the office space might not count formally as tenant participation, it can offer all kinds of opportunities for tenants to get to know how things work, and informally begin to influence what is happening around them. Not least, the presence of tenants can help to ensure that the whole organisation (not just front-line staff) has some contact with tenants.

Conferences

Most tenants said they had not been invited to any conferences or workshops organised by the support agency, although purely social gatherings were not uncommon. This is not to suggest that social events are not of great value or significance. For example, the tenants who had chosen to become members of their support organisation, and who had subsequently been to the House of Lords for a meal to celebrate the 50th anniversary of the support organisation, clearly felt included. However, given the way that many organisations use events like conferences and workshops as development tools, the failure to involve tenants in these activities appears to represent wasted opportunities.

In just a couple of services (both supporting people with learning disabilities) tenants mentioned activities which gave them an opportunity to meet and work with the wider staff body. For example, one organisation had set up some joint training, which was for both staff and tenants (something the tenants seemed to like):

'Yes, it was good.'

In both organisations, tenants had been able to attend and play an active part in a 'meeting' which turned out to be the Annual General Meeting (AGM). This had involved tenants

making a presentation to the meeting about their house, and the things they were working on at the time.

Contacts with the wider system and with user-led organisations

Again, very few of the tenants interviewed were able to describe situations where they had been involved in tenant participation activities targeted beyond the support provider. Almost all those who had, did so by virtue of belonging to a user-led campaigning organisation like People First. Those who had some contact with these organisations were keen:

'It's good, though sometimes people come late.'

One man spontaneously commented that the People First meeting he went to was better than the 'house meeting' because:

*'You can talk about **anything** [his emphasis].'*

However, relatively few of the tenants with learning difficulties had heard of People First, and even fewer of the users of mental health services had come across the network of 'Survivors' of psychiatric services. Of those who had not been involved, some responded to the idea with enthusiasm:

'Yes, I'd like that.'

Others, however, were indifferent to the idea of getting involved with such groups. As one commented, in relation to his mental health:

'This has been an issue now for thirty years. I don't really want to talk about it any more.'

Planning new developments

One or two tenants said they had been involved in developing plans for new schemes:

> 'We have a meeting with
> the deputy directors.'

Typically, these meetings took the form of a small planning group, meeting on a regular basis. The emphasis seemed to have been on trying to learn lessons for the future from the experiences of existing tenants:

> 'We talk about what is good,
> and what we don't like.'

For those involved, the sense of making an active contribution appeared to provide a lot of satisfaction, an issue picked up at the end of this chapter.

Challenging the service: the right to complain

> 'Oh, I wouldn't make a formal
> complaint. I don't like any trouble.'

These are the words of an otherwise very articulate tenant. Complaints procedures represent a crucial mechanism for tenants should things go wrong. As **Chapter Four** shows in more detail, all the organisations represented in this study had some form of complaints procedure in place. However, as the remark from the tenant suggests, the mere existence of the procedures does not guarantee they will be used. Indeed, knowledge of these procedures amongst tenants was very patchy. For example, when asked if it was possible to complain if something went wrong, a number said it was not. Further, when those who thought that it was possible were asked who they could

complain to, most only named immediate support staff.

There were a couple of exceptions to this rule. There was an awareness on the part of a small minority of tenants that they could complain to the Notting Hill Housing Trust. One tenant also mentioned that there was an annual visit by someone from the local authority inspection unit:

> 'I've met her. She makes a
> point of speaking to everyone.'

Even within houses, the knowledge about, and understanding of the procedures varied between tenants. One particular house illustrates the point particularly well. It was part of an organisation which had done more work on complaints procedures than most, and even to the casual visitor, the complaints leaflet was clearly visible. One of the tenants living in the house was able to describe the procedure in some detail, and claimed to have used it several times. However, another tenant in the same house said she felt she could not complain about anything. Even where good, well-developed complaints procedures exist, the message that people have a *right* to complain needs to be continually reinforced; the subject needs to be revisited on a regular basis.

Tenants were also generally unable to say where they might get help with a complaint, apart from front-line support staff. This reliance on front-line staff will be fine in many instances, but does leave tenants vulnerable. What happens if the support staff themselves are the source of the problem? There is a danger that the success or failure of complaints procedures will be determined entirely by the quality of the relationship between tenants and support staff, particularly if tenants have little sense of an organisation behind the local staff. There need to be other checks and balances in the system, a subject which is raised in both of the next two chapters.

Where tenants had used the complaints procedures, it was often to complain about the behaviour of other tenants. This is scarcely surprising. Notting Hill's own survey of tenants had suggested that this was a major issue for people, while other research has suggested that the commonest complaint about communal settings is likely to be about fellow users of the service (see, for example, Simons, 1993). The actions of people who live in the same house (or who live in close proximity) can make a huge difference to the tenant's quality of life. Yet this is an issue which, for a variety of reasons, services find difficult. This can send the wrong messages to tenants:

'I complained about another tenant, but nothing happened.'

While many tenants felt staff were very approachable, and that if you went to them with a problem you would be listened to, this was by no means a universal experience. In one service, for example, the catering arrangements were the source of vociferous criticism:

'They ask you about special diets, but don't cater for them.'

'It's Hobson's choice. There's only a vegetarian option if you tell them beforehand.'

'It was macaroni cheese three times in a row, followed by cauliflower cheese!'

'There's curry, but it's not black man curry, you know!'

Furthermore, the dissatisfaction with the food had become bound up with friction between the tenants and the cook:

'It's the way he [the cook] speaks to us.'

'He makes different food for himself.'

Attempts to raise these issues with the immediate management of the service had just led to further tension:

'They don't respond.'

From the discussion, it became clear that the service was uncomfortable with personalised complaints about specific members of staff. Yet this was precisely what was upsetting some of the tenants and, as a result, they had become convinced that management would always side with staff. The situation was complicated by the fact that the catering arrangements had been altered some months previously because of pressure from tenants. However, by virtue of the short-term nature of that particular service, that change reflected the views of a previous generation of tenants. The result was an unsatisfactory stalemate:

'It's like I've no right to complain.'

The Tenant Participation Initiative

Disappointingly, relatively few of the tenants interviewed had been directly involved in events organised as part of the Notting Hill Tenant Participation Initiative. The original survey of tenants' views appeared to have receded into history, and was remembered only vaguely by a few tenants. However, even the more recent events were known about by only a quarter of the tenants. To a degree, this is not surprising since a substantial proportion (again about a quarter) of those interviewed had only taken up their tenancies relatively recently. Some tenants had chosen not to be involved, largely because they did not like 'group' events:

'No, I do my own thing.'

However, equally some tenants from a range of services made it clear that they had never been told about the Initiative:

'Not heard of it.'

Those that had been involved with the user-consultants were very positive about the experience:

'Yeah, it was good.'

'There was a meeting for staff and tenants. It was interesting. They talked about their experiences.'

'They came to our meeting. We asked them questions, and they asked us some questions…Oh yes, it was good. When are they coming again?'

'I can't remember the details now, but there were lots of ideas.'

Opting out?

There were areas where a number of tenants said they were 'not bothered', and were quite happy to leave many decisions to professionals or the organisations who employ them. For example, one man commented that he thought it was better that tenants did not choose staff because:

'It would be a beauty contest.'

He also felt that the organisation was in a much better position to choose new tenants

because the professionals involved would have a much better knowledge of all the different factors to take into account. However, all the tenants interviewed at some point expressed an interest in participation that was not, at the time, on offer. To follow up the example of the man quoted above, when asked if he would change anything if he were in charge, he replied:

'I think a visit from the bosses would be good, to see their faces.'

One area in which many otherwise unenthusiastic tenants were interested was 'advising' the organisation about new schemes. Perhaps it was the way the questions relating to this issue were phrased, but even tenants who were otherwise reluctant to question or challenge the service appeared to like the idea of working *with* professionals:

'I would like to make a contribution.'

'You do care about how things are for other people.'

'Oh, I'd be happy to offer advice.'

This is a significant point. What at times may seem like apathy on the part of some tenants is probably more likely to be a combination of the accessibility and appropriateness of the participation options open to them and people's sense of identity. While some people are keen to challenge the system, for others such an attitude would be more or less unthinkable, whatever the need for such a challenge. If we learn one lesson from the tenants, it is that many different ways of participating are needed, and that what suits some, will leave others cold.

Chapter Four
The Views of the Professionals

It is not just tenants who have a legitimate interest in tenant participation. Professionals, and the organisations they work for, have a major responsibility for supporting and developing tenant participation. Indeed, tenant participation is often as much about meeting the needs of the organisations as it about enabling tenants to have more control over their lives. This chapter looks at the experiences and attitudes of the professionals towards tenant participation, along with the strategies for developing it established by the different organisations. Many of the issues raised in the previous chapter are followed up from this very different perspective.

In all, fifteen professionals were interviewed. The object of the interviews was partly to explore how professionals view tenant participation, focusing both on areas which they found difficult, as well as those they considered a success. At the same time, the aim was to explore the broader strategies used within these support organisations. How comprehensive was their approach to tenant participation? What kind of profile does tenant participation have within the organisation? These are some of the questions this chapter is designed to answer. The semi-structured questionnaire used has been converted into a checklist of issues, and is included on page 67.

As noted in *Chapter One*, the people interviewed played a wide variety of roles, from front-line staff to senior managers. They represented eleven very different organisations, including residential homes for people with learning difficulties (the biggest single group, four in all), several different services for people using the mental health system, short-term accommodation for single vulnerable people, a refuge for women and children escaping violence, and a drug-rehabilitation service.

The structure of this chapter follows the pattern established in *Chapter Three*. It starts by exploring tenant participation at the house level, before expanding outwards to take in the wider context.

Tenant participation at house level

Not surprisingly, tenant participation was most well-developed at the local level. All of the organisations were able to point to a significant range of areas where people were either involved in decision making or, in the case of the low-support services, where these matters were entirely in the hands of tenants.

However, *all* of the organisations had their weak spots. Involvement of people in many of these areas would be fairly uncontentious. Therefore the surprising thing is that *any* organisation was not giving tenants the opportunities to have a say in these issues. For example, two of the services did not offer tenants any choice of holiday. Similarly, two organisations failed to give tenants any say in the purchase of furnishings or fittings, or with decoration. One offered no choice of menus. One way of helping to decide menus is to be involved in shopping for food, yet there were a number of services where staff did all the shopping. In three services, tenants had not been involved in deciding the house 'rules'.

Some areas of activity within the home may not usually be classified as 'tenant participation', yet involving tenants, or giving them some responsibility in this area, could be important to them. There were still a few services where tenants did no cooking or washing up, all cleaning of communal spaces was done by staff, or where laundry was done in a large commercial machine which the tenants were not allowed to operate.

To reiterate, all these examples represented 'exceptions to the rule'. For each issue, the vast majority of services took some degree of participation in these areas more or less for granted. However, there were similar areas where a much larger number or organisations failed to involve tenants. For example, *none* of the organisations had consulted tenants in the process of setting service charges. Even though many houses had small budgets held at a house level for things like 'activities', in only three services was any degree of control delegated to tenants.

Similarly, most utility bills were paid by services without any participation by the tenants in the process. This last might not be the most exciting of options, yet including people in the process might have a number of possible benefits, including helping people develop skills and knowledge that they would need if they were to live more independently, and enabling them to have a better understanding of how *their* money is being spent. As one member of staff recognised, there was still a strong tendency for staff to:

'...*do things for people,
rather than with people.*'

There was also a tendency for participation to stop arbitrarily once a particular point had been reached. So, while most people were helping to choose colour schemes, in the majority of services they did not help to plan maintenance, even though decorating or repairs could be very disruptive to people's lives.

Finally, there were two important areas where only a minority of services were trying to open up involvement. These areas were:

● **Participation in developing job descriptions and recruiting staff**

What staff do matters to tenants. Having a role in the definition of job descriptions would be one way of enabling people to start defining the kinds of support they need. Yet in only one service involving people living in a smaller house, where the service was more individualised and there was more scope for flexibility, was this issue being discussed with tenants. However, even if tenants did not have direct input in this area, it did not always follow that they had no influence. One manager mentioned almost in passing that it had become clear that many tenants put a high value on nice food, and that, as a result, the organisation had put much more emphasis on cooking skills in job descriptions.

Only three services had mechanisms for involving tenants in recruiting front-line staff, although a few others allowed for some opportunities for tenants to meet prospective employees at the time of interview, and their views were informally 'taken into account' by the professionals.

● **Involvement in selecting new tenants**

A similar picture emerged in relation to the issue of choosing new tenants. As Notting Hill's own survey of tenants had recognised, the behaviour of other tenants can have a major impact on the quality of life for people in supported housing. However, this is genuinely a difficult area for services. Many, as a matter of principle, want to be an inclusive service with 'zero rejection'. (Who would provide for people who were seen as difficult to live with?) Others are not in a position to turn away 'business'. They cannot afford to leave voids, and the reaction is largely to take the people nominated by purchasers. As a result, more than half the services simply had no process (formal or informal) for involving people in tenant selection. Yet, as some of the professionals were only too aware, at times this was a major issue for some tenants:

> '*When he heard this man was coming to live here, he was absolutely terrified.*'

As a result, a number of the people interviewed did acknowledge that in exceptional situations they would listen to what tenants said to them, and would make judgements accordingly. However, this was often a haphazard process. In just one instance was there a clear and transparent process. For example, in one service, prospective

tenants would come to stay for a short while and the matter would be discussed at a house meeting before any final decision was made.

Keeping a wider vision

By definition, checklists will never cover all possibilities. The manager of one house commented that the most significant event within the house over the last year had been the illness and eventual death of one tenant. Helping the remaining tenants through the process of mourning had probably been the main priority of staff (who themselves had had to come to terms with their own feelings). Every effort had been made to keep the tenants involved as much as possible in making the arrangements following the death. For example, they had had to find a plot for the grave and to raise money for a headstone:

> '*It was about them helping to look after a friend in both life **and** death.*'

Apart from demonstrating a sensitivity to the important issue of bereavement, this example is also important because it underlines the importance of a wider vision in relation to 'tenant participation'; all important life events (of any kind) must be on the 'participation agenda'.

House meetings

Even if it was not part of an official policy, most houses were clearly expected to have house meetings, though in some cases these had fallen by the wayside:

> '*It's meant to happen, but with the lack of staff there has not been one for a long time.*'

As noted in **Chapter Three**, the approach to house meetings varied greatly on a number of different, overlapping dimensions. Some were a forum that was expressly for the tenants while some were dominated by staff. There were considerable differences in their formality; while some were really a social gathering, others were advertised in advance, chaired and minuted. Finally, while some were open to any interested tenants, others were more or less compulsory (even if there were no clear rules, tenants were often 'expected' to attend). In the latter case, the compulsory element was said to be necessary as the house meetings played a sort of rehabilitative role:

> '*They [the tenants] came here because they are basically in a mess. They need a bit of structure to help them sort themselves out.*'

> '*It helps them start taking on some responsibilities.*'

There were mixed views about the success of the house meetings. The professionals from services where tenants had taken a much more active role tended to be the most positive. For example, the following comment was made in a house where staff could raise issues but only as 'any other business' at the end of the meeting, the bulk of the meeting was explicitly for tenants:

> '*It has been a very gradual success. It has grown over the three years it's been going. Getting the tenants to set the agenda and to take over chairing the meeting helped move things on.*'

This rather positive view of house meetings contrasted with opinions expressed by a couple of staff who felt that house meetings were, by and large, not working. Both of these situations involved settings where the meeting was largely run by staff. Given this, their complaints that tenants 'never raise issues' and were 'too passive' were not entirely surprising. However, it has to be added, there were other situations where house meetings were primarily led by staff which were considered to be 'successful'. What emerges is a rather muddled picture. House meetings actually played different roles in different contexts, yet there was often an impression that the main reason they existed was because staff felt there *had* to be one, without always being clear why.

Individual planning

Most of the services had some process for regularly reviewing the support offered to each individual tenant. These were perhaps most developed within the learning-difficulty services, where there is a strong tradition of 'individual planning'.

Once again there were very clear differences in the approach of the various organisations. For some, individual planning was very much something for the individual tenants. For example, in one service, tenants themselves were said to have control over the agenda of any planning meetings as well as who attended; the resulting care plans were written jointly between the tenant and the keyworker, and each tenant would keep a copy of their own plan. In another, workers and tenants were said to make joint assessments, tenants were encouraged to define their own goals, and care plans included a section on accountability completed by the tenant and not seen by keyworkers. However, many of these features were missing in other services. Individual planning largely seemed to consist of formal assessments done by *staff*.

Nevertheless, even where there was an emphasis on involving tenants, there were still sometimes frustrations that the individual planning had not always acted as the catalyst for the change intended:

'People [staff] don't put their thoughts about development in a structured manner...it's not functioning as it should; there's nothing coming out of it...It's still back at basics. There's no "Where does this lead?".'

Inclusive or exclusive?

One of the dangers with tenant participation is that it will be seen as the preserve of more articulate tenants. Some people, particularly those who have multiple impairments, or little or no speech, risk being excluded.

The consequences of excluding people were spelled out by one member of staff working in a house for people with profound learning difficulties. She described how a purpose-built building had been commissioned from a group of architects. Despite the fact that the brief had specified that the building was to be wheelchair accessible, some of the doors were too narrow for powered chairs, and in some of the rooms there was insufficient space for chairs with larger turning circles.

As a result, this organisation now involves existing tenants directly in the commissioning of new services. Architects are invited to meet and get to know tenants, often resulting in a much more imaginative response to design questions. Tenants get to tour buildings as they are being built, highlighting any potential problems with access as early as possible. Even though the tenants who have been involved in this are not people who can articulate their views through speech, it is just as much 'participation' as any other form, and has made a significant contribution to improving new developments.

Staff in this same establishment have also worked very hard to make sure that even tenants with the most profound disabilities still have as much involvement in decisions as possible. They work on the principle of:

'If she could say, I'm sure she would want more control.'

Here, tenants' reactions to situations and events are interpreted as communication; staff watch people's behaviour carefully for clues as to what the individuals wish. For example, after a period it became clear that one of the tenants was eating more at lunchtimes than in the evening. As a result, the house switched the main meal of the day to lunchtime.

Every attempt was made to ensure that everyday activities were structured so as to enable people to participate as much as possible. Again, taking the tenant mentioned in the previous paragraph as an example, staff discovered that she found it a lot easier to choose her own clothes if the rack on which they were kept was lowered, and if the clothes were kept in the same order.

In this context, the skills and the commitment of staff are crucial:

'After a time working with individuals, staff do build up a picture of what people do and do not like. We try hard to maintain the continuity of staff.' ■

The involvement of the tenant's friends and family in planning was an area that was generally not well developed. As suggested in **Chapter Three**, the contact that tenants have with the wider world is often very important to them. Involving friends and family in planning ought to be part of any strategy designed to help tenants build on those wider links, but most organisations either failed to have any mechanism for this, or took an essentially passive approach to the issue:

> *'There's no clear role [for family and friends]. If users want, we invite them [to the planning meetings].'*

There were, of course, exceptions. One service did have a family services worker whose role was to provide some active liaison with families. Another service, provided as part of a hospital-resettlement programme, had been aware of opposition to hospital closure amongst families, and had set out to work with them on their reservations about community care. As a result of this, the service felt they had been able to make some 'converts'.

There are genuine questions about how to involve families and other people from the community in planning around individuals without undermining the autonomy of the tenants themselves:

> *'What you want is general support from families. If they get involved in planning, it can cause difficulties.'*

However, involving tenants and involving their friends and families are not mutually incompatible. Indeed, failing to involve families in planning can leave individuals feeling very isolated and under great pressure at times of change (Booth, Simons and Booth, 1990).

Tenant participation within the support organisations

Without exception, all the professionals interviewed felt the prime responsibility for developing tenant participation lay with the support providers, although some did acknowledge that NHHT had a legitimate role in 'monitoring' tenant participation (see also the Box below, **Housing and support, or rehabilitation?**).

Housing and support, or rehabilitation?

One particular organisation had the most difficulty fitting into the standard housing and support model. The house included in the study offers a medium-term option for unsupported families and children as part of a drug-rehabilitation programme. The house is organised on the principle that at any time ex-drug users are always outnumbered by people who have never been users. The tenants, therefore, include less experienced staff who live-in for a given period, along with a 'support group' of tenants who simply live in the house alongside the ex-users, and who go out to work at a range of 'ordinary' jobs during the day.

The house operates a number of rules which would not necessarily be in place in other services. For obvious reasons the house is strictly drug-free. The co-ordinator estimated that about a third of tenants get asked to leave immediately because they fail to keep to this agreement (they only have licences, not assured tenancies). The organisation runs three different houses, but has generally kept them quite separate as a matter of policy; in the past relationships across houses caused complications if tenants were asked to leave.

The rules around visitors are also quite complex and unusual. While visitors are generally encouraged (parents and partners can come and stay) this welcome does not extend to ex-drug users:

'It's difficult in drug rehabilitation. You [the ex-user] can't go back to the people you knew — that would mean going back to drugs — you need to build up new links.'

Attendance at the regular house meetings is expected — the house has a very strong emphasis on collective decision-making — although the co-ordinator acknowledged that missing the odd one was not a problem.

Because they are so small, there are few formal structures, and most things are done by word of mouth. Generally the tenants are articulate, and apparently rather suspicious of anything that smacks of 'officialdom' (they chose not to be involved in the tenant participation events or the research). For example, the co-ordinator mentioned that the house had an equal opportunities policy which the staff tended to be keen on, but which the tenants disliked:

'They see it as a means for us to try and control them — to stop them buying The Sun.'

With tenants living alongside staff, and with the mediating influence of the support group, many of the traditional barriers between workers and tenants get broken down. As a result, in the view of the co-ordinator, tenants have a lot of control over what happens within the basic framework of the service offered.

As the co-ordinator of the service pointed out, drug rehabilitation services have been hard hit by the community care reforms over the last few years and many services have had to close. As a result, the organisation felt under considerable pressure:

'We get big demands from Notting Hill and the local authorities. There's a lot of form filling. We are a very small organisation trying to keep our own identity.'

Some of the pressures include an expectation of the service to adopt tenant participation structures which, the interviewee felt, had been developed within very different areas and which do not reflect the way this particular service works. Not that the need for some monitoring by NHHT is disputed. Rather, tenant participation is one of many factors which are seen to be pushing an unusual (and, in the view of those involved, valued) service in more conventional directions. ■

Indeed, within some organisations there was some resentment of Notting Hill's proactive approach. In two instances this was partly because organisations felt they were being forced to go in directions which did not reflect the real nature of the service they offered (see the Box opposite: **Knowing what you are about: organisational aims and tenant participation**). However, there was also a feeling in some quarters that tenant participation was being given too high a profile by Notting Hill in the face of many competing pressures. So, for example, some houses that would have been included in the scope of the research declined to take part. This was said to be partly because the tenants involved were not interested, but also because the staff working within them were said to be suffering from 'participation fatigue'.

Given this emphasis on the role of the support organisations, surprisingly few had taken steps at a strategic level to promote tenant participation. Fewer than half of the organisations had a formal policy on tenant participation. Only one had a member of staff with a specific remit to develop tenant participation within the organisation, even though professionals in some of the other services recognised that this lack of focus meant that many initiatives got lost. For example, one manager commented:

> 'Our previous experience was that we talked about tenant participation but nothing got off the ground until a consultant came in, did some work, and made sure it was followed up.'

Similarly, the majority of organisations had no budget identified for developing tenant participation. This does not necessarily mean that no resources could be found. For example, the interviewees were asked whether tenants could access funds to attend conferences or events organised outside the organisation. The majority thought it would be possible. Similar answers were given to questions about the possibility of tenants obtaining financial help towards training and materials about tenant participation. Finally, most organisations felt they would be able to provide some practical help if tenants wanted to organise meetings or events on tenant participation, including the use of office space and equipment. However, a number of those interviewed made it clear that so far there had been 'no demand' for such resources — although of course tenants would probably not have been aware of these possibilities.

There is a wide variety of ways in which to organise tenant participation at an organisational level, both in terms of the processes and structures used, and substantive areas where tenants could reasonably expect some involvement. Some of the more important areas are set out in the rest of this section.

Part of the organisation? Membership and Annual General Meetings

All of the services represented in the study were effectively not-for-profit entities. At least half of them could be categorised as 'membership' organisations; supporters of the organisation can become 'members', and, in theory at least, the Board of the organisation is accountable to the wider membership. In some cases, members are able take part in the regular election of Trustees. The crucial question here is: can tenants become members of the organisation in their own right?

Effectively, the membership organisations split down into three roughly equal groups: those where tenants were clearly eligible to join; those where they were not eligible; and

Knowing what you are about: organisational aims and tenant participation

In her report, *'It Seems Like Common Sense to Me': Supported housing tenants having a say*, Monica Keeble contrasts the way in which the stated aims of many organisations appear to be all about tenant participation, with the way in which, in practice, tenant participation is perceived to be a sort of optional luxury; in the words of one person quoted in the report:

'The icing on the cake.'

Once again the findings from London have strong echoes of those from Wales. The majority of those interviewed unambiguously described the organisational aims in terms which suggested that tenant participation should be a cornerstone of the service:

'Supporting people to have a big role in the decisions of their own life.'

'To enable the individuals to…fulfil their own goals…and to open out experiences.'

There were only a couple of staff whose interpretation of the aims of the organisation made no mention, implicit or explicit, of tenant participation:

'The most effective thing is to get a roof over heads.'

'Provide a safe and secure environment.'

On the whole, those who stressed tenant participation most explicitly tended to work in contexts where the issues were most to the forefront, and where tenant participation appeared to be taken most seriously. Equally, those organisations which did not to appear to have participation as a recognised corporate goal tended to be those where the issues of participation were least well developed. In this sense, it would not be true to say that there was a total dislocation between the aims of the organisations and what they actually did. However, it is the case that reality seemed to fall short of aspiration; organisations are often bad at distinguishing between how they would like things to be, and how they actually are. This was recognised by a few of the professionals interviewed:

'There are some barriers. There are limitations in being a registered care home; it's not their own home… That's another compromise. What is some people's home is other people's workplace.'

Nobody said outright that tenant participation was not important although, by implication, it was clearly not seen as a high priority in several services:

'It's finding the time to do it…'

Only a few of the organisations involved appeared to have fully followed through the logic of their 'mission statements'. For a variety of complex reasons, what are presented as key principles do not get translated into the design of services. ∎

those where tenants could qualify for membership after a certain period (for example, two years). However, in at least a couple of organisations, this last option had the effect of dividing tenants along the lines of the service they used:

> '*I think the tenants in the registered care home get invited...but not the tenants in the short-term accommodation.*'

In a couple of services where people moved on, it was possible for ex-tenants to become members, but in general short-term tenants are effectively discriminated against.

Similarly, Annual General Meetings (AGMs) represent an important opportunity for the organisation to be held to account, and for the organisation as a whole to meet and look ahead. In a few services (mostly for people with learning difficulties), groups of tenants had an active role to play at the AGM (for example, making a presentation), but mostly, even if they were present, tenants did not appear to have a significant profile at these events.

Involvement in formal decision-making bodies

Just one of the organisations in the study had a current tenant on the management board, and even here this was a recent development. In another two, tenant representatives were able to observe the management committee meetings but were not able to vote, and in two more services there were one or two ex-tenants involved in high-level committees.

This was, however, an issue that had clearly been raised in several organisations and, although often strongly supported by the staff interviewed, it had not actually happened for reasons, including:

- **Concerns at board level**

At times the blockage seemed to be at the top of the organisation, amongst existing board members:

> '*There has been an initial lack of confidence at Council [the Organisation's Board] level. As trustees they are liable...*'

- **Lack of enthusiasm from potential tenant representatives**

Equally, there had not always been much enthusiasm or pressure from tenants:

> '*There were no takers for it, but it would have been very intimidating.*'

In this case, there seemed to have been no attempt to make it *less* intimidating by adapting the process for tenants.

- **Concerns about representation**

In most cases, the assumption appeared to have been that that there would have been only one or two committee places allocated to tenants. In the organisations with more diverse groupings of tenants (particularly those that provided both short- and long-term services) there was the inevitable question of who would speak for whom:

> '*There would be potential conflict between the different groups of tenants.*'

- **Worries about 'tokenism'**

People were worried about not getting it right first time:

> '*We don't want it to be tokenistic.*'

Involvement in planning new developments

Services often work the way they do for historical reasons. It is harder to change what exists than start afresh on a new footing. New developments often represent a real chance to change the service offered in ways that would reflect the views of tenants. Unfortunately, it was an opportunity only really taken up in three of the organisations. For example, one service set up small planning groups around each new develop-ment, and interested tenants were included in these groups.

There was often an assumption that the people who should have a say in new schemes would be the people who would eventually live in them. However, prospective tenants were often identified only quite late in the process, which meant there were whole areas of the planning process which by-passed them. Occasionally, attempts by the service to find out what potential tenants wanted resulted in established plans having to be torn up. For example, one manager pointed to the occasion where her organisation was asked to develop a home for eight people with learning difficulties, only to discover that all the tenants being proposed by the local authority actually wanted to live some-where smaller. Despite much of the rhetoric about basing services around the needs of individuals, most services develop 'schemes' — and then try to find people who will fit into them.

Tenancies and participation

According to the professionals interviewed, tenants covered by the research could be split into two roughly equal groups; those who had assured tenancies and those who had licences. Since the latter offer considerably less security to tenants than the former, this is a matter of concern. There are some circumstances where a licence is appropriate (for example, in the case of the refuge for women and children escaping violence), but in many instances the use of licences appeared to reflect the organisation's fears about the nature of the security of funding for support staff more than any other reason. One or two professionals were rather hazy as to whether tenancies or licences were in place, but since the two forms of agreement confer quite different rights to the tenant, this confusion is a matter of some concern.

Tenants' groups

The opportunity for tenants from across an organisation to meet and discuss issues was another idea that less than half of the organisations had followed up, and the opportunities that did exist often turned out to be relatively limited (for example, the AGM was cited as a forum for tenants to meet in a number of cases).

The formation of a service-wide tenants' association had been considered in one instance, but as the manager in that service explained, the plans had hit a philosophical barrier:

'Are we saying there should be one? That would be like management saying there should be a union.'

One organisation had got as far as helping to establish a small residents' association for tenants in three local supported-housing schemes that were built on one site, even though the three were all run by different support organisations. According to the person being interviewed, this had initially seemed really promising, but the initiative had eventually fallen apart:

'Everything took so long to do. There was a small amount of money available and the residents asked for a bench and a sleeping policeman. But after a year nothing had materialised. Just nothing came of it.'

Conferences, workshops and training

'We set up an event to look at day services. People First facilitated it and tenants were involved.'

Most of the services organised regular conferences, workshops and other training events for staff. Relatively few included tenants in these activities. These are wasted opportunities. This is not to suggest that tenants will need or want to attend everything an organisation sets up; rather that it simply does not make sense to exclude tenants when thinking about areas of future development and change. This is partly because tenants ought to have the chance to get to hear about and have a say in these issues, and partly because they have valuable knowledge and experience to contribute.

As the quotation above suggests, there were some imaginative examples of what can be done. For example, a couple of other services had joint training on things like health and safety, first aid, and food hygiene, where tenants and staff could learn alongside each other.

The user-led consultancies demonstrated just how effective training by people who use (or have used) services can be, yet only one service had taken up this model. Here a tenant with learning difficulties had got involved in developing the 'lifestyles' planning that had become the main vehicle used by the organisation to plan around individuals.

This tenant had then gone on to help train staff in how to use the planning manual produced, taking increasing responsibility for the training as he became more experienced. In addition, he had started to produce a newsletter for staff and tenants on the subject, which in turn offered a space for other tenants to contribute material. Within the same organisation, three tenants had also trained volunteers. Perhaps the most significant development was that on occasions tenants had been paid on a consultancy basis for their contribution to staff training.

Evaluating services

There were examples of services that were subject to an annual review by senior management, and in a couple of instances this included opportunities for tenants to meet those carrying out the review. However, this was not always something the tenants felt confident about:

'There is a annual management inspection, and the tenants are offered confidential interviews, but then senior managers are not exactly familiar figures.'

However, this was still an essentially passive role for tenants. There was just one organisation which talked of a more active role for them, but even here it was still very much in the planning stages:

'We are in the process of introducing a system of annual review. This will involve the service users directly. Initially this will build on their existing contributions to annual reports and the AGM, but eventually we hope they will be playing a full role alongside staff.'

Tenant participation:
an equal opportunities issue?

One of the aims of the study was to discover to what extent organisations had adapted tenant participation structures to allow for the diversity of tenants. For example, what steps had been taken to open up the tenant participation process to people from minority ethnic groups and non-English speakers? How were the views of gay and lesbian tenants recognised? How was access to the process ensured for non-readers, people with a sensory impairment, or people with a physical impairment?

Most of the professionals struggled with these questions. This was partly because clear participation structures of any kind were few and far between. However, it was also because some of these questions simply did not seem to have been considered. For example, a number of the organisations had no established access to translation or inter-preting services. Most had no way of providing information in Braille. Many organisations had premises which were not physically accessible.

It is true that a number of those interviewed thought that steps could be taken 'if needed' (for example, bringing in sign-language inter-preters). However, once again this represents a very passive attitude to what are important issues. How will these needs be articulated if these groups are marginalised within the service?

There were, of course, positive examples where organisations had considered at least some of these issues. For example, one had consulted extensively in the local minority ethnic community and, as a result, had estab-lished a women-only house for people from local Asian families and had set out to recruit

Punjabi-speaking staff. At least some (though by no means all) of the learning-difficulty services regularly produced information on audiotape, or produced information in more accessible forms (an issue returned to later — see below). One organisation had involved gay and lesbian tenants in writing its policy on sexuality. One organisation had a policy that all meetings should be on accessible premises. However, these were the exceptions rather than the rule.

Producing accessible information

Giving tenants the basic information about their rights and options might reasonably be seen as a key part of any tenant participation strategy. Many of the services had taken some initial steps in this direction. For example, just over half had talked to tenants or user organisations about the images and languages used by the organisation:

'We had discussions with People First...'

'We talked about this within the house.'

Similarly, most services provided a range of information to people. However, this range was rarely comprehensive, nor, in many cases, was the information provided in a format that was useful to tenants.

Most services provided three basic documents: a copy of the **licence or tenancy agreement** (all services), **a tenant's handbook** (all but two), and a **complaints leaflet** (all but three — see comments on p47). The tenancy agreement and the handbook were often recognised as documents that were either not accessible to tenants, or little used (which suggests that even if tenants can read them they do not find them useful), although both had been targeted by a couple of services (particularly those supporting people with learning difficulties) for further work.

Just over half the organisations provided a breakdown of service charges, but the other documentation covered by the questionnaire was only provided by a *minority* of services. Quite a number gave tenants details of support contracts, which explained the kinds of support they might expect, although there was some doubt about how informative these documents really were. Few had any kind of service 'charter'. Although most services had an open-records policy, under half of them gave tenants information about how to access files as a matter of course. Similarly, not many tenants would have had information about the structure of the organisation (for example, names of senior managers) nor, even amongst those which encouraged it, would they necessarily be told how to become a member of the organisation. Some services provided a copy of *The Tenants' Guarantee*, although again this is not a document that many tenants find easy to read. Slightly more positively, just under half of the services did provide a regular newsletter about the organisation, and some of these did include contributions by tenants.

However, in contrast, few of the services had made material about participation widely available to tenants.

Rather startlingly, there were examples of organisations which produced information, but did not, as a matter of course, give it to tenants. The most remarkable instance of this involved a service charter!

Much of the information for tenants was provided on their arrival in the services. This means that just when people are in a situation where they are least likely to be able to cope with it, they get overwhelmed with material,

much of which is not particularly meaningful to them. There seem to be few mechanisms for making sure this information is re-visited at a later date, or reinforced in any way.

Perhaps not surprisingly, staff in the services for people with learning difficulties were most attuned to issues of accessibility. However, it is not only people with learning difficulties who have difficulties with formal documents; accessibility ought to be an issue in all services for vulnerable people.

In most cases, where documents were not particularly accessible, there was an expectation that staff would 'go through' them with tenants. However, there often appeared to be little monitoring to see if this actually happened. In fact, this is expecting a lot from front-line staff. Making documents simpler and more straightforward helps staff explain issues. It can be difficult to explain complicated or technical concepts clearly, and it is unrealistic to expect front-line staff automatically to be good at this.

Involvement in recruiting management staff

While there were few enough services involving people in the recruitment of front-line staff, there was only one where tenants had helped select staff in some sort of management position. Here, at least, the issue had been taken seriously. Tenants were provided with some training on selection and equal opportunities issues, were involved in the shortlisting process, and took part in the interview panels.

Challenging the services

'*They [senior management] like the idea, but they would throw their hands up in horror if someone actually made a complaint.'*

All the services included in the study had some form of complaints procedure. However, they varied immensely both in their comprehensiveness and how much the staff being interviewed knew about them.

Some of the services had clearly invested some time and thought into the development of their complaints procedures. For example, in one house, the staff member being interviewed was able to locate a complaints leaflet, and was able to describe very clearly the choices that tenants had when complaining. Within the organisation, this included being able to choose whether the matter was dealt with by a house manager, or whether it 'jumped' straight up to the more formal stages of the procedure, where it would be investigated by senior managers. Alternatively, residents could go outside the organisation and enlist the assistance of either the local inspectorate or NHHT. The same member of staff was also able to point to a number of sources of independent support for people who wanted to complain, including a list of advocates, a housing advice service, a self-advocacy group and a free legal service, all with contact numbers.

In contrast, for others, the complaints procedure consisted of a few lines in the back of the tenant's handbook which did little more than assert that tenants could complain if they wished. Some of the staff interviewed were also alarmingly hazy about the options open to tenants, at times saying little more than that tenants were always able to complain through staff. In other cases, tenants had to ask for the complaints leaflet; it was not automatically supplied to all tenants.

The questionnaire included an additional question about mechanisms for ensuring that, if tenants are issued with a notice to quit because of an alleged breach of tenancy agreement/licence, they are able to challenge the grounds for the notice.

In a number of services there seemed to be no real protection for tenants in this situation. Therefore, while some organisations allowed appeals to the chief executive or to the board, others said that the main way for the tenant to question what was happening was through the legal system:

'I assume that they would go to a solicitor. It does suggest it on the licence.'

Of course this assumes that people know that they have a right to go to court. As at least one interviewee acknowledged, with startling frankness, that most tenants do not know their rights:

'Some people give you grief and you have to get rid of them. Even as it is they could sit tight, but they don't know it.'

Tenant participation in short-term tenancies

More than any other group, tenants with short-term tenancies seemed prone to being excluded from tenant participation.

They often were not around long enough to get involved in some of the strategic developments. By definition, they have least motivation to look at the long-term future of the service, and the services they used often appeared to put the least emphasis on tenant participation.

Some obvious opportunities were being missed. For example, there was the case of the organisation where the cook operated a standard fortnightly menu. This had been altered once because of tenant pressure, but there was no attempt at regular consultation which, given the short-term nature of the services involved, might well have helped form the basis of some further dialogue.

This lack of involvement of short-term tenants was recognised by two services, who are beginning to develop some 'exit' participation (in one case an interview, in the other a survey) for tenants leaving the service.

Tenant participation within the wider system

As one member of staff commented, organisational boundaries pose a problem for tenant participation:

'We often find ourselves supporting tenants in areas like finding work, but we have to do that within the boundaries of being a care organisation overseen by the Borough.'

Following the logic of this remark (one that was echoed by staff from other organisations), any comprehensive strategy on tenant participation would therefore include trying to find ways of helping tenants influence the broader system. However, as far as it was possible to tell, this approach was not on the agenda of most organisations.

There were, of course, exceptions. The manager of one house described how a number of members had been on protests and rallies organised by the disability movement, and had even been to the House of Commons to lobby MPs. The issue of voting had also been taken very seriously in this particular house. At the time of the 1992 general election, the tenants had written to all three parties to try to find out their policies in relation to services for people with learning difficulties. Labour and the Liberal Democrats replied to the letter with an acknowledgement and a promise of further information, which in both cases failed to materialise. The Conservative Party did provide a more detailed response, but managed to alienate the tenants by its tone!

In another instance, an organisation had paid for a tenant to join an 'action learning set' organised by the National Development Team for people with learning difficulties, designed to promote the idea of supported living (people living in their own homes; see Simons and Ward, 1997).

Finally, one of the houses from one organisation had been built as part of a small estate, most of which was general needs housing. One of the tenants had joined the local residents' association formed on this estate and, with appropriate support from staff, was now on the management committee. He had been able to raise a number of issues of concern to his fellow tenants, including complaints about the behaviour of local children. This issue had been taken up by the residents' association. Here was such a positive example of what tenant participation could be about, yet it involved just one house from the many operated by these eleven organisations.

Independent advocacy

Probably one of the most empowering opportunities for many users of supported housing (or indeed, other services) has been the opportunity to access some form of independent advocacy, either in the form of a self-advocacy group (Simons, 1993a), by having an independent advocate (Simons, 1993b), or even being part of a circle of support (Wertheimer, 1995).

Tenants from three of the four learning-difficulty services were members of People First. In at least a couple of these services there were active links between these independent user-led groups and the services. For example, as indicated earlier, People First were helping one organisation rewrite their tenant participation strategy. Membership of People First was also one opportunity for tenants to get involved in wider campaigns about services, and there was often active encouragement from professionals for people who had joined, along with practical support to get to meetings.

Similarly, one organisation, along with NHHT, had actively supported the development of an advocacy project in a local volunteer agency precisely because they were aware of the potential for conflicts of interest for professionals employed by the service:

> '*We felt it would be wrong for the advocacy worker to be based in [names own organisation].*'

Similarly, following the events organised as part of the Tenant Participation Initiative, another organisation had developed links with a local citizen-advocacy organisation.

However, even where there was a recognition that independent advocates were a good idea, there was often frustration at the difficulties in finding enough people to take on this role. The majority of organisations appeared to see encouraging the development of independent advocacy in any form as outside their remit. As a result, most of the organisations acknowledged that there was little opportunity for tenants to access independent support of any kind.

The Tenant Participation Initiative

Somewhat startlingly, some of the professionals interviewed had no direct knowledge of the NHHT Tenant Participation Initiative. Of these, some had only joined the organisation or changed role recently. In other instances, it emerged that staff who had been involved in the user-led workshops had only been temporary:

> '*It was the agency staff who went.*'

They had subsequently moved on and taken their knowledge with them.

Those that had been directly involved were generally positive about the experience:

> '*It was a good learning experience.*'

Some had come back reinvigorated and enthused:

> '*Yes, we have used it to look at what we are doing.*'

> '*It was a shot in the arm... re-fired my vision.*'

> '*It was really good to be in an environment where everybody shared the ideals of tenant participation.*'

This had been despite the fact that some of the issues raised during the events were potentially challenging for staff:

> '*I did have some awkward feelings initially, but I thought it was really good. It highlighted some of our limitations.*'

> '*It challenged some long-standing organisational blocks, pushing on things that had started...*'

Staff could also point to the impact on tenants:

'*More people are going to People First, partly at least because of their involvement.*'

'*The tenants took the report from [the user-consultants] to the Borough.*'

There were, however, some reservations expressed, often reflecting the varied response of tenants to their involvement:

'*People picked up on having a voice, but it frightened a few people — stirred up some memories [of being in an institution].*'

'*They [the tenants] had an odd reaction. They didn't really take to it.*'

This did not necessarily imply any criticism of the user-consultants. For example, one professional commented that seeing the user-consultants had really inspired some of the tenants, but also added:

'*I suspect some tenants don't identify with empowered people.*'

This was also reflected in the feeling that the user-consultants were not typical of the tenants in the services in question:

'*It was led by articulate, insightful tenants. We are working in an environment where tenants don't present themselves as articulate. It's a very slow process building up their confidence.*'

This particular interviewee had been directly involved in the meetings of the *Good Practice Guide* group (see **Chapter Two**):

'*I'm hoping something will come of the good practice guidebook. I would like to see a wedge of it directed at the users who we work with.*'

As some staff recognised, the problem for the organisations was picking up where the events finished and maintaining the momentum:

'*I think its usefulness was limited because of its one-off nature.*'

There was perhaps an inevitable tendency for those who were most enthusiastic to also be those who had already been working on the issues:

'*We were able to say a lot of the things were going on here.*'

'*It confirmed some of the things we were doing.*'

'*Things had been slipping. It reinforced the message to keep things up.*'

Some of these enthusiasts were only too aware that the Initiative would not always be as welcome elsewhere, even within the same organisation:

'*I know they did not get invited to the house where it might have been a new message.*'

The apparent apathy of some tenants towards participation

In her report on tenant participation in Wales ('*It Seems Like Common Sense to Me*'), Monica Keeble found that the biggest barrier to tenant participation was often said by professionals to be the apathetic attitude of the tenants themselves. She herself refuted this, pointing to a considerable unmet demand for more involvement amongst tenants. Just as this last finding was echoed in this research (see the end of **Chapter Three**), so, too, did some staff comment negatively on the failure by some tenants to take up opportunities to get involved.

There was evidence of a frustration that at times more progress had not been made:

'People have got so far and then stood still.'

'The tenants have yet to realise the full potential for change.'

At times, this lack of interest from tenants was said to be in stark contrast with the enthusiasm of some professionals:

'To be honest, this is an issue that has excited staff more than the tenants.'

Some of the interviewees sounded as if they were on the verge of 'blaming' tenants for the lack of progress in tenant participation. There was certainly the odd interviewee who was frankly critical of tenants:

'It's the fact that people here are in a mess...They have no sense of discipline... They lack the knowledge of how to conduct yourself...'

However, in most cases, those interviewed turned the issue on its head and presented it as a reflection of the 'failing' of staff to understand the tenants' perspective:

'I have been frustrated when users don't show enthusiasm. But then that's probably because of my lack of empathy with their experiences.'

Barriers to further development

The overall impression is that, despite some pockets of good practice, many of the services have failed develop a coherent tenant participation strategy, particularly at an organisational level. As one interviewee acknowledged, the chances of tenants having an influence on major issues were limited:

'They can say things through the house meeting, but bigger issues, no.'

Given the importance attached to promoting participation in much of the official guidance on services over recent years (much of it, admittedly, a matter of vague exhortation rather than specific guidelines), this lack of development is something of a surprise. Why is this the case? What barriers are there to developing tenants' participation?

There was actually remarkably little consensus amongst the professionals interviewed about where the main blockages were. For example, some of the houses that had been doing work on tenant participation at a local level saw the organisation as one of the main barriers for further developments:

'We are generally ahead of the rest of the organisation. It has become a bit of a tension. We have had to wait for the rest of the organisation to catch up. For example, we had plans to individualise the tenant's handbook, but we had to put it on hold because of the need to get it approved by the Trustees.'

However, equally, there were people at the centre of the organisation who saw some of the front-line staff in the houses as a source of resistance:

'There is only so much we can do. We can set things up, but it is up to staff in the houses to take them up.'

Other barriers identified by professionals included:

● **Complexity**

Some respondents felt that part of the problem lay in the complexity of the issues, leaving the whole area prone to misunderstandings and misinterpretations by both staff:

'It's difficult to get staff to grasp the issues.'

and tenants:

'It's OK with practical immediate things, but they have got no strategic view.'

'It's easier with day-to-day practical issues. Helping the tenants understand some of the organisational issues can be difficult. It can be hard to find the right medium.'

● **An overly passive approach**

Several interviewees commented that they thought many professionals tended to be too passive in their approach; they waited for tenants to raise issues, rather than actively presenting information and options to tenants:

'We should be more proactive in consulting people: "How can we improve things?"'

● **Inertia**

'It's difficult to do. At times it is simply easier not to do it — though people won't admit it.'

None of these barriers appear insurmountable. As has been repeatedly pointed out throughout this and the earlier chapters, there are models of good practice in a whole range of areas. The question is how to encourage services to see tenant participation as a higher priority.

Chapter Five

What Kind of Vision? Reflections and recommendations

This report is based on a premise which can be summed up in the phrase:

'Nothing about us without us.'

In other words, **tenants should have a say in any matters which affect them, directly or indirectly**.

This does not mean to say that all tenants will want to be involved in everything (in fact, it is pretty clear that they will not). However, the *opportunities* for involvement should be there. Further, the fact that at times tenants will choose *not* to get involved does not invalidate the principle; people should be able to opt out of participation structures without forfeiting the right to opt back in at a later date. This means making sure that opportunities are regularly presented to people, even if they are not initially taken up.

Nor does it mean that services should do everything that tenants demand. Services do not just have to be accountable to tenants, they are bound by all kinds of other obligations, not least the need to conform with the requirements of purchasers' statutory regulations. Inevitably, professionals will have to retain responsibility for making many decisions, based on their judgement of how best to balance all the potential conflicting demands. However, those decision makers need to ensure that the voices of tenants are heard, and must be willing to account to tenants for the decisions they make. Tenants, after all, are the reason why the service is there.

A second, related assumption that underpins this report is that **tenant participation should be driven by what matters to tenants**, rather than simply reflecting the way that services are organised. Given that the services often loom large in the lives of people who use supported housing, there will be a lot of overlap. However, people's lives do not begin and end at organisation boundaries. By implication, tenant participation should not be just about matters internal to the service.

A third assumption is that **there are inherent conflicts of interest** for both organisations and the individual professionals involved. While many of the staff interviewed as part of this research were clearly very committed to tenants, there are limits to the extent to which they can or will genuinely 'empower' tenants to challenge their own practice or the actions of their employers. There has to be independent support for tenants when they want it. Similarly, independent tenant-led organisations have a potentially vital role to play.

The final key assumption is that, reflecting the very different skills, experiences and attitudes of tenants, **there needs to be lots**

of ways for tenants to get involved; the process of enabling tenants to have influence needs to be more varied and imaginative. At a local level, there are often different options for tenants to have some influence over what is happening, but at higher levels within the organisation the routes narrow down. Here there is likely to be an emphasis on formal structures involving tenants' 'representatives'.

An interesting account of the difficulties of establishing tenant participation based on such mechanisms in the context of supported housing for women escaping domestic violence is available in Warren (1996).

While representational structure will probably have a part to play, it needs to be made to work effectively (see the box **Who speaks for whom?** below) and to be balanced by other avenues for tenants to have an influence at this level.

Who speaks for whom?

Not surprisingly, where there are models of participation based on formal represen-tational structures, there are arguments about who speaks for whom; some of the things tenants say get discounted because they are seen to be 'unrepresen-tative' of the wider tenant body.

There are lots of conflicting considerations. For example, *on the one hand:*

- **Representation gets confused with typicality**

Good representatives are often atypical people. Just because someone is not a typical tenant does not mean that they are of necessity out of touch with how most tenants feel about a subject.

- **Tenants find themselves caught in a Catch-22**

If they are articulate, their views are seen as 'unrepresentative'; if they are not articulate, then their views get discounted anyway.

- **Tenants' representatives and tenant-led organisations get judged by double standards**

For example, any personality clashes or power struggles in user-led organisations are interpreted as evidence of the incapac-ity of tenants to behave appropriately, as though such things never happen in professional organisations.

- **Tenants who speak get criticised**

Tenants are often criticised by professionals who believe they know more about how other tenants feel, but who have actually never talked to the other tenants about the subject in question; these professionals 'represent' no-one but themselves.

- **Professionals tend to define 'constituencies' in service terms**

They then refuse to work with indepen-dent user-led groups based outside the service.

On the other hand:

- **Representing others effectively is a very demanding job, which requires all kinds of skills**

Not everyone has those skills. Many people find it much easier to speak about their own lives rather than reflect the experience of others.

- **Relying on formal representational structures effectively excludes many tenants who could make a contribution**

- **Sometimes tenants' organisations try to 'speak for' tenants in ways which really do not reflect their interests**

- **Where tenants have very diverse views or interests, it can be very difficult for one or two representatives to speak on their behalf.**

Formal representational structures can be very important. However, they need to be made to work by everybody involved:

- **People need to have support and resources to be an effective representative**

- **The more organised the constituency, the easier it is for people to represent it**

- **Organisations need to have more than just one or two tenants' representatives, and a process for ensuring that marginalised groups are included (for example, by having reserved places for representatives of minority ethnic tenants or tenants with disabilities).**

Of course, one way around these dilemmas is to involve people because they are interested, or because they have a skill to offer, or because they have something to say. Above all, tenant participation is not synonymous with involvement in committee meetings; the mechanisms used to involve people should reflect not just the needs of the organisation but the strengths and wishes of the tenants. ■

The picture that emerges from the research does not match up to these four assumptions about how things ought to be. This is not to say that there were not good examples of innovative practice. On the contrary, some organisations, or rather the individuals within them, had clearly been very imaginative, and were undoubtedly genuinely committed to working *with* tenants. These examples show what is possible. While tenant participation may not be an easy option for organisations, raising as it does all kinds of complex dilemmas, it clearly is possible to make it work.

However, the examples of good practice were all too often exceptions rather than the norm. The overall impression remains that the principles of tenant participation are more talked about than acted upon. Indeed, the way that tenant participation was implemented tended to be:

- **As a low priority**

While all of the organisations involved in this research accepted that they bore a substantial responsibility for developing tenant participation, the majority appeared to have taken relatively few steps towards really discharging that responsibility, often having no policies on tenant participation, nobody with a brief to focus on the issue and no identified resources. Clearly, for many organisations, tenant participation was not anywhere near the top of their agenda. This is not to suggest that those responsible for running those organisations were necessarily against the principles or the practice of tenant participation; rather, these issues just did not seem to be a priority in the daily press of competing demands.

● **Confused in its aims**

There seems to be some confusion over where tenant participation begins and where the rehabilitative strategies adopted by the services end. As a result, some of the things that got categorised as 'tenant participation' seemed to be as much about staff trying to shape the behaviour of tenants, than about tenants having a chance to shape the service. If compulsory house meetings run to staff agendas are important as part of a planned programme of 'treatment' (and it was not always clear that this case could be made) then these same meetings should not be also seen as 'tenant participation'. There should be some alternative opportunities for tenants to influence what is happening.

● **Narrow in scope**

So much of what is happening remains focused on very limited areas within individual houses. There was often little sign of a wider vision of tenant participation. There were whole areas of the workings of the services which tenants remained largely unaware of or uninformed about, let alone involved in.

In addition, the way services respond to the kinds of concerns expressed by tenants suggests that 'tenant' participation' is often seen in terms which are too narrow, too concerned with helping the tenants to make the best of what is available, rather than helping them to change services in fundamental ways.

At this point it is worth adding a caveat. There are dangers of undervaluing small-scale local opportunities for people to have more control over their lives. Many of the enthusiasts for tenant participation were most excited by the tenants getting involved at high levels within the organisation (for example, getting on the board) or doing things which challenged people's perceptions of tenants (like having tenants as trainers). Yet take the example of the tenant described in *Chapter Four*, who found it easier to choose her clothes once staff had worked out how to organise things in a way that suited her. For that tenant, this simple act probably made a big difference to her life. *All* levels of participation can be equally important.

● **Inward-looking, based on a service-dominated agenda**

Finally, the inevitable conclusion of the interviews with both tenants and professionals is that too often tenant participation has been driven by the concerns of services. As a result, most of what happened was inward looking. The support for tenants to begin to get involved with the wider system seemed to be largely absent.

In short, what seemed to be missing in most services was a coherent strategy to make tenant participation really work. The next section of this chapter explores the elements that might make up such a strategy.

Tenant participation: a strategic approach?

One certain finding from this study is that none of the organisations represented were doing everything they could. On the whole,

User-led structures

Many ideas that are considered in mainstream tenant participation — for example, tenant co-operatives as managing agents — rarely, if ever, get discussed in relation to supported tenants.

There are dangers of making assumptions about tenants, and their perceived incapacities, which simply do not hold up on closer scrutiny. There are instances of entirely user-led services (the various Centres for Independent Living — CILs for short — are cases in point) or of tenants, or potential tenants, playing lead roles within organisations.

One example of the latter is an organisation called SWALLOW* (see Simons, 1995b) a small housing project based in Midsomer Norton for local people with learning difficulties. The project involves people in a number of ways. There is an 'interest group' which is open to all people with learning difficulties in the area. The interest group then elects representatives onto the management committee, which also includes families and professionals, as well as one or two people from the local coalition of people with disabilities. People with learning difficulties actually make up more than 50% of that management committee. Finally, two people with learning difficulties are employed by SWALLOW as part of the project team. The result is an organisation which is largely user-directed. ■

---

this is not surprising, and many of those involved would argue that they were well-aware of their shortcomings, that it is impossible to do everything at once, and that they had established priorities for taking things further. They also might add that no sensible organisation could conceivably do everything suggested below; that would overwhelm tenants and staff alike.

All this is true. While there are no grounds for complacency, even for those organisations which take tenant participation seriously, there needs to be some sense of proportion. The elements set out below are not meant to be a prescriptive list to which all services should sign up at once. Rather, it represents an attempt to set out a wider vision of what tenant participation could be about. However, the risk of being overwhelmed is greatest when tenant participation is seen as something distinct and separate. It is much less likely to be an issue where the principles are embedded in the service; when support is provided in a participatory way.

One way of easing the pressures on services would be to allow for much greater collaboration and sharing of ideas across organisational boundaries. Many of the things suggested in this report will be beyond the scope of small organisations acting on their own. To take a specific example, it can be very demanding of time and energy to produce good-quality accessible information. However, there is no need for each organisation to continually reinvent the wheel.

Possible options for avoiding this duplication of effort include:

- larger partnership organisations (like NHHT) providing a 'clearing house' for

---

* SWALLOW stands for South Wansdyke Learning and Living Our Way.

examples of material which can then
be adapted

- organisations forming consortia
to develop shared material

- adapting material that is in the public
domain (see *Resources* on p73).

Similarly, there needs to be an acceptance
that small organisations do not need the
same levels of formal structures and process
which are required in larger organisations.
This should not, however, be at the cost of
diluting tenants' rights.

People in short-term accommodation

It emerged clearly from the research
that people who are living in short-term
accommodation are a 'marginalised'
group as far as tenant participation is
concerned. In such services, any participation strategy will have to be adjusted
to rectify this.

For example, there may well need to
be:

- a much stronger emphasis on making
accessible information readily and

continually available to people; this
would include information about
move-on options

- a means of ensuring that the service
is as flexible as possible, so that each
new generation of tenants can adapt
it to their needs

- the use of 'exit' interviews or surveys

- immediate membership of the
organisation which continues after
the individual has moved-on

- greater opportunities for ex-tenants
to get involved. ■

The precise details of any strategy designed
to make tenant participation work will vary
with the particular context, but the following
components all have a claim for inclusion:

- **Involvement of tenants in
developing the strategy**

Tenant participation should reflect the
concerns of tenants, in terms of both substance and process. The only way to ensure
this is to involve them from the word go.

- **A clear policy**

The aims of tenant participation should be
set out, and put clearly in context within
the overall priorities of the service.

- **A 'tenant participation person'
(or persons)**

There should be identified individuals
within the organisation who will take
responsibility for developing tenant
participation.

- **A tenant participation budget**

This should include resources to pay
tenants for the work they do when
appropriate.

- **A mechanism for ensuring
diversity is recognised**

There should be mechanisms within the
tenant participation strategy which take
account of the varying interests and

concerns that will exist amongst tenants, and which guarantee that steps are taken to ensure that the voices of otherwise marginalised groups among the tenants are heard.

- **Maximum possible control for tenants in their own home**

At an individual level, there should be opportunities for self-assessment by tenants, chances for tenants to discuss the kinds of support they want, and a recognition of tenants' wider aspirations. Where those aspirations are not reflected in the current service, there needs to be established mechanisms for staff to help tenants articulate those aspirations in the appropriate system (for example, to care managers). Collectively there should be involvement in appointing new staff and selecting new tenants. In both cases, this should be done in an open and transparent manner with appropriate safeguards built in.*

- **Opportunities for tenants to develop a collective voice**

There needs to be space for tenants to get together on their terms, and establish their own agenda, both at a local level and in the wider context.

- **Opportunities for tenants and staff to work together at a local level**

There were often few opportunities for tenants and staff to sit down and work

together as equals. One possible model for this kind of framework is the quality assurance group (see Millner, Ash and Ritchie, 1991).

- **A clear presence within the organisation for tenants**

Tenants should be eligible for membership of organisations. Similarly, they should have a clear presence in the 'offices' of the organisation, allowing opportunities for informal direct contact between tenants and decision-makers at all levels. An interesting example of this kind of approach is the Ling Trust, based in Colchester. Here there is a tenants' association open to all Ling Tenants, which meets in the board room. Tenants who want to find paid work are also employed as cleaners within the office, and have a status as 'staff' alongside the other Ling employees.

- **Involvement of tenants in decision-making structures at all levels**

See the box **The issue of tokenism** overleaf.

- **Well developed complaints procedures**

See the box **Effective complaints procedures** overleaf.

---

* For a detailed discussion of the issues around involving people who use services in the selection of staff, see the material by Townsley *et al.* listed in the **Resources** section.

The issue of tokenism

Chapter Four showed that some of the organisations had begun to explore the possibility of including tenants on the board, but had baulked at the idea because of concerns about 'tokenism'; they felt that to simply have one or two tenants on the board would be more about being seen to involve tenants rather actually doing it.

Like many of the debates on the subject, there are arguments both ways. There is, of course, some substance in the concerns. It is certainly true that many tenants would find the typical board meeting an intimidating and probably alienating experience. There are also all the issues about representation explored earlier in this chapter; it is going to be very hard for one or two individuals to effectively represent all tenants.

However, there are things that can be done to improve the situation. By adapting meetings to the needs of tenants, they can be made more participatory; rather than assuming that it will be 'business as usual', the meetings have to change, for example, by:

- becoming less formal (dropping things like addressing the meeting through the chair, dwelling on points of procedure, and the like)

- breaking the meeting up into shorter sections, so that people do not have to endure long sessions without a break

- making sure that tenants are always welcomed, and that everyone introduces themselves and explains who they are

- making sure that the purpose of each meeting is clearly explained

- having all the papers for the meeting in accessible formats, preferably sent out to tenants well in advance

- tenants being briefed during and after the meeting about what will/is/was happening

- tenants having supporters available whose whole role is to facilitate their effective involvement

- organising the meeting in a way which ensures that tenants have an opportunity to contribute, and that items of interest to them are not kept until the end of the agenda

- avoiding all jargon, and properly introducing and explaining all issues.

The paradox is that, far from inhibiting the work of committees, many of these steps can have the effect of making them better for *everyone* involved. Of course, it is also possible to go the whole hog. Many of these problems simply do not arise in user-led organisations, where tenants are embedded in the whole structure.

However, not many of the organisations included in this study are likely to become user-led in the foreseeable future. Indeed, getting any people on to a board at all could be an important step forward. Tokens can be an indication of good intent. Provided organisations are prepared to learn from the mistakes, things can move forward. Being frozen into immobility because of concerns about tokenism could be the worst option. Not least, if the tenants involved are prepared to do dramatic things like resign from the board in protest if it fails to offer genuine participation, then it may be possible to get across the message about the need to change! ■

Effective complaints procedures

On reflection, the complaints procedures were one of the weakest areas of tenant participation reflected through this research. While there is extensive material about complaints procedures in the NHS (Wilson, 1994) and Social Services Departments (SSI, 1991; Simons, 1995), there has been much less discussion of these procedures in the context of supported housing within the independent sector.

The discussion documents produced by the Citizen's Charter Complaints Task Force (CCCTF, 1995a and b) on complaints procedures in public organisations provide some valuable advice, but any comprehensive complaints procedure should probably include:

- **Clear, accessible information** (developed, of course, with tenants) and given to tenants as a matter of course; this information should:

  - explain that tenants have a right to complain

  - provide reassurance that tenants will not get into trouble for complaining

  - indicate where tenants could get help to complain

  - provide explanations of options within the procedure, including the right to miss out informal local stages, rights to access the complaints procedures established by landlords, the local authority social services department, and other appropriate external bodies

- **Straightforward information for staff,** highlighting the role in helping tenants access the complaints procedures

- **An informal stage** where complaints can be handled locally with an emphasis on conciliation or mediation; however, this stage should be optional — tenants should have the right to go to more formal stages from the outset

- **A more formal stage** where any investigations are carried out by trained staff who do not have direct management responsibility for the part of the service complained about; if necessary or appropriate, outside investigators might be used

- **A clear right of appeal** to the governing body/chief executive of the organisation

- **A named person** responsible for receiving and co-ordinating complaints within the organisation; this person should be accessible to and known by tenants (for example, their name, telephone number and photograph should be in the complaints leaflet)

- **Liaison with complaints officers** in housing providers and local authority social services departments, including agreements on how to support tenants across organisations

- **Mechanisms for recording and analysing complaints** across the organisation

- **Procedures for establishing how satisfied complainants were with the response of the organisation**, even if they do not take the complaint further

- **Opportunities to identify the wider lessons for the organisation arising from complaints** — including identifying areas where tenants appear to be unable to access the process — through, for example, an annual audit of complaints

- **Access for tenants to independent support** to help them complain; this is probably best developed by the organisation in conjunction with the local authority or on a cross-organisation basis

- **Care procedures for staff**, including clarification that people who are the subject of a complaint will be supported through the process; complaints procedures and disciplinary procedures should be clearly separated out

- **Whistle-blowing guidelines** for staff who have serious concerns about the treatment of tenants

- **Clear alarm-bells** within procedures which, when triggered, result in immediate high-level consideration of issues

- **Acceptance of third-party complaints** 'on behalf of' tenants, including consistent handling of complaints regardless of who is making them

- **An immediate acknowledgement of all complaints**, and subsequent full responses, delivered within specified timescales

- **A clear set of established options for redress** (which should include the possibility of individual and corporate apologies, and compensation where appropriate). ∎

- **A clear role for tenants within the organisation**

Options here would include involving interested tenants in:

- working parties planning new developments

- evaluating services

- accessing joint training alongside staff

- providing training, with appropriate support.

- **Accessible information**

The checklist on page 67 spells out areas where information might reasonably be expected by tenants. Wherever possible, information should be in written and non-written forms (for example, audiotape and/or video).

- **Access to independent support**

This needs to take a number of forms, including independent advocates, and assistance and encouragement for tenants to get involved with independent self-advocacy groups or tenant-led organisations.

- **A framework for tenants to participate within the wider system**

See the box **Influencing the wider system** opposite.

The role of the housing provider

During the last two chapters, the spotlight has been largely away from the Notting Hill Housing Trust itself. Since the Tenant Participation Initiative was set up at their instigation, it is appropriate to end the report by reflecting on their role.

Influencing the wider system

One way for tenants to influence what happens around them is for them to get involved in the political process. Tenants may legitimately expect to be able to:

- vote

- join political parties

- lobby their representatives at a local and national level.

Similarly, there is a range of organisations whose policies are going to directly affect them, and which they may want to seek to influence, wherever the opportunity arises. For example, tenants might want to get involved in, or be consulted about the development of:

- the community care plans produced by social services departments

- strategies established by the local health authorities for mental health and learning-difficulties services

- statements of housing need produced by the local strategic housing authority.

In each case, there should be forums for tenants to access in relation to these policies.

There is one important organisation missing from this list. The Housing Corporation (and its Welsh and Scottish equivalents) had a key role in the development of supported housing. The policies of the Housing Corporation do have implications for tenants. However, although part of the Housing Corporation's remit is to promote tenant participation, it appears to restrict its role to exhorting others, rather than practising what it preaches itself. Professionals from the Housing Corporation did attend a tenant participation event organised as part of the Tenant Participation Initiative, so it is not as if the Corporation is not interested in the issues, but, until recently, there have been no established mechanisms for tenants to influence the Housing Corporation directly. Things are changing though: in response to concerns expressed by a number of organisations, the Housing Corporation has provided funding to a consortium of six housing and support organisations to enable them to produce an accessible version of the Corporation's recent discussion paper on supported housing, and for them to consult widely with their tenants on the Corporation's proposals. This is a one-off exercise. However, it is hoped that this will herald a rather more active role in tenant participation on the part of the Corporation in the future. ■

As an organisation, NHHT clearly saw part of its role as ensuring that the rights of tenants were recognised by their partner agencies, focusing in particular on tenants' rights to participate. The Tenant Participation Initiative was set up to stimulate developments in this area. Undoubtedly, in some respects the Initiative was very successful. Things happened because of it, and in general it bumped the issue up the agenda of many organisations.

However, there were also some frustrations. Some of the organisations involved had an unerring capacity to diffuse any momentum generated by the Initiative; for example, by sending agency staff to training days or by not passing on the information to tenants.

Some appeared pretty reluctant to hear the message.

As suggested in **Chapter Four**, there were strains between the perspective of NHHT and some of the partnership organisations over the issue of tenants' rights. The example of the rehabilitative services which asked tenants to sign up to rules which waived some of their rights as tenants is a case in point. This poses a dilemma.

On the one hand, as a matter of principle, people should not have their rights limited. On the other hand, if the services which take the form of rehabilitative communities offer something to the people concerned that they would not get elsewhere, then they should not be precluded by an absolutist approach to the issues.

The answer to this dilemma will depend on one's view of the value of those particular services. However, as Monica Keeble comments in her report, it is important to be clear about conflicts between people's rights as tenants, and additional clauses inserted into agreements that limit those rights. If, for example, people are given the chance to enter some form of therapeutic community where they accept rules and restrictions that would not normally be part and parcel of a tenancy agreement, then this should only happen on the basis of informed consent; they should know what they are foregoing. Furthermore, it seems right that the organisations involved should be held to account, and have the opportunity to justify and explain the way they work. While there is an argument for some degree of flexibility in the way services are organised, it seems proper that social landlords like the Notting Hill Housing Trust, in their role of protecting people's rights, should be questioning these issues, even if they subsequently accept the

arguments of those offering the therapeutic community approach. In other words, a degree of tension between housing and support providers is probably healthy; the relationship should not be too cosy. Indeed, there are some commentators who argue that the clear separation of housing and support services represents a form of protection for tenants (see, for example, Kinsella, 1993).

As was noted in **Chapter Two**, NHHT argued, perhaps rightly, that it could not impose conditions on its partnership agencies. However, there is scope for negotiations, and social landlords might reasonably seek some of the following conditions in partnership agreements, particularly where larger support organisations are involved:

- the existence of an appropriate tenant participation strategy, with agreed monitoring of progress

- a clear statement of the rights of tenants

- an agreed budget for tenant participation

- minimum standards for the provision of information about tenants' rights and participation (some of which will need to be provided by the landlord).

There was also the matter of access to information for tenants. Some of the support agencies controlled all the contacts with tenants. At one level, as a matter of confidentiality, it is perfectly reasonable for support organisations to protect the privacy of tenants. However, it was clear from the interviews that some tenants never got information intended for them. This was probably more a question of cock-up than conspiracy, but nevertheless it is a problem; effectively, people were denied information about their rights. Monica Keeble identified the same problem in Wales. As a matter of principle this seems wrong. Moreover, structurally it is dangerous. Without implying anything negative about the organisations included in this study, having a situation in which tenants largely have contact with just one organisation leaves them vulnerable. People will be better protected where the landlord has direct contact with tenants, including the capacity to send people information without it being filtered by support organisations. The following items could therefore reasonably be added to the list of things that need to be addressed within agreements between housing providers and their partnership organisations:

- reasonable direct access to tenants

- mechanisms for ensuring that the housing provider can provide tenants directly with information

- the right to invite tenants to workshops, events or training. without the messages being filtered out.

Of course, many of the elements of the tenant participation strategy listed above might reasonably be expected from housing providers, as well as managing agents or support providers. Indeed, tenants could expect both sides of the housing and support divide to work collaboratively on many issues, otherwise there is a risk that important opportunities will slip down the gap. Although many of these issues had been considered by NHHT, not all of them had been fully addressed.

To finish with, it is worth returning to just one of the original aims of the Initiative: getting tenants from supported housing involved in the mainstream participation structures established by the Notting Hill Housing Trust. That original aim got overtaken by events. Not unreasonably, other issues became to be seen as a higher priority. However, the lack of involvement in these structures mean that supported tenants lost out on the opportunity to have any influence over mainstream housing; housing which they might wish to use at some stage as an alternative to conventional 'special needs' provision, either as a move-on option, or as part of a 'floating support' (see Morris, 1995) or 'supported living' (see Simons & Ward, 1997) package. Excluding supported tenants from these structures risks ghettoising them.

Having said that, the question remains how to find ways of helping supported tenants to start making the leap across the boundaries. Again the examples provided by Monica Keeble make it clear that it is possible. In her view, one of the keys to this is supported tenants having a much more active role in their communities. It seems reasonable to assume that any strategy to achieve this aim would include:

- an audit of key community projects and organisations

- practical support for supported tenants to play a role in these organisations, including transport, child care and so on

- providing forums for supported tenants and mainstream tenants to meet and discuss issues

- adapting mainstream structures to make them more inclusive.

A Checklist on Tenant Participation Issues

General ✓

▶ Has the overall responsibility for tenant participation issues been discussed and established amongst the different organisations involved in the service you provide? ☐

▶ Does your organisation have a tenant participation policy? If so: ☐

  ● Were tenants involved in developing it? ☐

  ● Are tenants involved in reviewing it? ☐

▶ Do you have staff who have a specific responsibility for the development of tenant participation in your organisation? ☐

▶ Is there a budget for tenant participation? ☐

▶ Would the following be available:

  ● Bursaries for tenants to attend conferences or workshops outside the organisation? ☐

  ● Staff time to support people at such events if required? ☐

  ● Training for tenants on matters relating to tenant participation? ☐

  ● Funds for tenants to buy materials for tenant participation or self-advocacy? ☐

  ● Funds to cover the travel costs of tenants going to meetings or participation forums, self-advocacy groups, and the like? ☐

  ● Access for tenants to practical support in organising tenants' groups including access to office space and equipment? ☐

✓

- Funds to pay tenants for particular work done
for the organisation?

☐

Participation within the organisation

▶ Are tenants involved in the main decision-making bodies
in your organisation?
If yes:

☐

- Is there adequate support for these tenants'
representations?

☐

- Have the workings of these bodies been adapted to
the needs of the tenants or is it still 'business as usual'?

☐

▶ Are there forums in which tenants from across the
organisation can meet and discuss issues?

☐

▶ Can tenants become members of the organisation in their
own right?

☐

- If so, do they have the same rights as other members
to attend the AGM, vote, and so on?

☐

▶ Do tenants have an active role at the AGM?

☐

▶ Are tenants involved in:

- designing new schemes?

☐

- reviewing the images and language used within the
organisation?

☐

- choosing staff at all levels in the organisation?

☐

- training staff/other users of the service?

☐

- evaluating or reviewing services?

☐

- all quality assurance initiatives?

☐

▶ Are tenants automatically invited to conferences, workshops
or training courses organised by the organisation?

☐

Equal opportunities issues

✓

Are there mechanisms for ensuring that voices of minority groups are heard within the organisation, including:

- people from minority ethnic groups? ☐
- non-English speakers? ☐
- gay/lesbian tenants? ☐
- non-readers? ☐
- people with a sensory impairment? ☐
- people in short-term accommodation? ☐

Information

Do you automatically provide **accessible** material in the form of:

- a copy of the licence/tenancy agreement? ☐
- a tenant's handbook? ☐
- the tenant's guarantee? ☐
- a complaints leaflet? ☐
- a service charter? ☐
- job descriptions for support staff? ☐
- details of the organisation (who's who/membership, and so on)? ☐
- information about rights and tenant participation? ☐
- service charges? ☐
- newsletters about activities/new developments/events/ conferences? ☐
- how tenants can access their personal files? ☐

Complaints procedures

Do your complaints procedures meet the standards listed in *Chapter Five*? ☐

In particular:

- Is there independent support for people wanting to complain? ☐

✓

▶   ● Have the rights of tenants to access wider complaints systems been established and clarified? ☐

Independent advocacy

▶ Is it made clear to tenants that they have a right to join independent self-advocacy groups? ☐

▶ Is it made clear to tenants that they have a right to appoint an independent advocate? ☐

▶ Do you have clear policies for facilitating the involvement of people outside the organisation to take on an advocate's role? ☐

▶ Does your organisation actively support and encourage the development of independent advocacy organisations, including the provision of no-strings funding where possible? ☐

Participation at the 'house' level

▶ Do tenants have a say in:

● the job descriptions of support staff? ☐

● the recruitment of front-line staff? ☐

● the selection of new tenants? ☐

● the setting and use of house budgets? ☐

● house 'rules'? ☐
This would include:

– the use of communal areas ☐

– visitors ☐

– pets ☐

– decor? ☐

– furnishing? ☐

– equipment? ☐

– maintenance/refurbishment? ☐

– menus? ☐

– social activities? ☐

– holidays? ☐

✓

▶ Do tenants have the opportunities to participate in all aspects of the day-to-day running of the house, in particular:

- shopping? ☐
- cooking? ☐
- paying bills? ☐
- cleaning? ☐
- laundry? ☐

▶ Is there a forum for tenants to meet and discuss issues amongst themselves? ☐

If yes:

- Do tenants control the agenda? ☐
- Do tenants control the running of the forum? ☐

▶ Are there opportunities for tenants to meet and discuss issues with staff on an equal basis? ☐

▶ Are there mechanisms for ensuring each individual tenant has as much control over their life as possible? ☐

▶ Are there clearly established mechanisms for tenants to find out about alternative accommodation and support, and to pursue them if they wish? ☐

Participation in the wider world

▶ Are tenants supported to vote? ☐

▶ Are tenants supported to join in the wider political process? ☐

▶ Are tenants informed about relevant tenant-led organisations, and supported to become members if they wish? ☐

▶ Are tenants enabled to join mainstream tenants'/residents' organisations? ☐

✓

▶ Are there opportunities for tenants, should they wish it,
to be involved in:

- local community care planning?

- local housing policies?

- local policy development in the areas that affect them?

- the Housing Corporation?

☐
☐
☐
☐

Resources

Material referred to in the text

Booth, T., Simons, K. and Booth, W. (1990) *Outward Bound: Relocation and community care for people with learning difficulties.* Milton Keynes: Open University Press.

CCCTF (1995a) *Putting Things Right: Main report.* London: HMSO.

CCCTF (1995b) *Good Practice Guide.* London: HMSO.

Housing Corporation (1989) *The Tenant's Guarantee: Guidance on management by registered housing associations of housing accommodation provided in shared housing and hostels and for special needs in separate dwellings.* London: Housing Corporation.

Keeble, M. (1996) *'It Seems Like Common Sense to Me': Supported housing tenants having a say.* Cardiff: Tenant Participation Advisory Service (Wales) and Joseph Rowntree Foundation.

Kinsella, P. (1993) *Supported Living: A new paradigm?* Manchester: National Development Team.

Lindow, V. and Morris, J. (1995) *Service User Involvement: A synthesis of findings and experience in the field of community care.* York: Joseph Rowntree Foundation.

Morris, J. (1995) *Housing and Floating Support: A review.* York: Joseph Rowntree Foundation.

Simons, K. (1993a) *Sticking Up for Yourself: Self-advocacy and people with learning difficulties.* York: Joseph Rowntree Foundation.

Simons, K. (1993b) *Citizen Advocacy: The inside view.* Bristol: Norah Fry Research Centre.

Simons, K. (1995a) *I'm Not Complaining, But…Complaints procedures in social services departments.* York: Joseph Rowntree Foundation.

Simons, K. (1995b) *My Home, My Life: Innovative approaches to housing and support for people with learning difficulties.* London: Values Into Action.

Simons, K. and Ward, L. (1997) *A Foot in the Door: The early years of supported living for people with learning difficulties in the UK.* Manchester: National Development Team/ Pavilion.

SSI (1991) *The Right to Complain: Practice Guidance on Complaints Procedures.* London: HMSO.

Warren, F. (1996) *Supported Housing for Women Fleeing Domestic Violence: Developing tenant participation.* York: Joseph Rowntree Foundation.

Wertheimer, A. (1995) *Circles of Support: Building inclusive communities.* Bristol: Circles Network UK.

Wright, L. (1996) Taking it from us: training by people who know what they are talking about. In T. Philpot and L. Ward (Eds.) *Values and Visions: Changing ideas in services for people with learning difficulties.* Oxford: Butterworth Heinemann.

Other material of interest

Reports

Jeffrey, J. and Seager, R. (1995) *All Together Now: Involving black tenants in housing management.* Tenant Participation Advisory Service (England).

PCHA (1994) *Participation In Supported Housing: A good practice guide.* Available via TPAS, England.

Scott, F. (1996) *Setting Up a Tenants' Group.* London: Values Into Action.

Townsley, R. and Macadam, M. (1996) *Choosing Staff: Involving people with learning difficulties in staff recruitment.* Published in the **Community Care into Practice** series by The Policy Press in association with the Joseph Rowntree Foundation and *Community Care* magazine. It is available from The Policy Press, University of Bristol, Rodney Lodge, Grange Road, Bristol BS8 4EA. Telephone: 0117 973 8797. Fax: 0117 973 7308. ISBN 1 86134 0427. A summary of the research for people with learning difficulties is available free of charge as part of the **Plain Facts** series, available from the Norah Fry Research Centre (address below).

Townsley, R. Howarth, J., Le Grys, P. and Macadam, M. (1997) *Getting Involved in Choosing Staff.* A resource pack aimed at supporters, trainers and staff working with people with learning difficulties. Brighton: Pavilion Publishing Limited.

TPAS (1994) *Involving Tenants with Special Needs.* Tenant Participation Advisory Service (England).

Villeneau, L. (1992) *Housing With Care And Support: A quality action guide.* MIND.

Videos and training packs

Allen, P. and Scales, K. (1990) *Residents' Rights: Helping people with learning difficulties understand their housing rights.* A video and training pack. Brighton: Pavilion Publishing Limited.

Rural Media Company and Simons, K. (1997) *I'm Not Complaining, But...* A flexible training resource on complaints procedures (further details from the Norah Fry Research Centre). A video and training pack designed to encourage the use and development of complaints procedures in services for people with learning difficulties. Brighton: Pavilion Publishing Limited.

Slater, D. and Hughes, A. (1995) *Mary Complains.* A video and resource pack about making complaints for people with learning difficulties. Brighton: Pavilion Publishing Limited/Entelechy New Moves.

*See also VIA Direct Video Group and the People First Publications (under **Accessible material** below).*

Accessible material

NFHA, New Era, Penta (1995) *Your Tenancy or Licence Agreement: A basic guide.* National Federation of Housing Associations. (An accessible guide to help explain tenancy agreements or licences.)

People First (1995) *Helping You Get the Services You Want.* London: People First.

People First (1995) *Your Rights to Housing and Support* (two books and tape). London: People First. (Video made by people with learning difficulties exploring tenant participation.)

Scott, F. (1996) *Setting Up a Tenants' Group.* London: Values Into Action.

The Symbols Project.

A joint project between the Advisory Unit: Computers in Education and Borehamwood Day Centre, designed to improve communication through the use of symbols.

Address:
The Advisory Unit, 126 Great North Road, Hatfield, Herts, AL9 5JZ

http://www.rmplc.co.uk/eduweb/sites/advunit/

VIA Direct Video Group (1996) *It's My House: Your rights as tenant.* London: Values Into Action.

Wilcox, H. *Pictures for Choice: Involving tenants with special needs.* Tenant Participation Advisory Service. Photocopiable pictures for use in tenant participation.

Addresses

Joseph Rowntree Foundation
The Homestead
40 Water End
York Y03 6LP
Tel: 01904 629241
Fax: 01904 620072
http://www.jrf.org/

National Housing Federation
175 Gray's Inn Road
London WC1X 8UP
Tel: 0171 278 6571
Fax: 0171 833 8323

Norah Fry Research Centre
3 Priory Road
Bristol BS8 1TX
Tel: 0117 923 8137
Fax: 0117 946 6553
E-mail: Norah-Fry@Bris.ac.uk
http://www.bris.ac.uk/Depts/NorahFry/

Notting Hill Housing Trust
Windmill House
10 Windmill Road
London W4 1SD
Tel: 0181 563 5000
Fax: 0181 563 4599

Pavilion Publishing
8 St George's Place
Brighton
East Sussex BN1 4GB
Tel: 01273 623222
Fax: 01273 625526
E-mail: pavpub@pavilion.co.uk

Tenant Participation Advisory Service
(England)
Brunswick House
Broad Street
Salford M6 5BZ
Tel: 0161 745 7903
Fax: 0161 745 9259

Tenant Participation Advisory Service (Wales)
2nd Floor
Transport House
1 Cathedral Road
Cardiff CF1 9SD
Tel: 01222 237303
Fax: 01222 345597

Values Into Action
Oxford House
Derbyshire Street
London E2 6HG
Tel: 0171 729 5436
Fax: 0171 729 7797
E-mail: VIA@BTInternet.com
http://www/demon.co/via/

Appendix

Details of the research

Of the 36 organisations working in partnership with the Notting Hill Housing Trust (NHHT), 12 were initially selected for inclusion in the research on the basis that they represented the wider range of experiences found in NHHT-supported housing. All 12 were approached through a formal letter from the NHHT explaining the nature of the research and seeking the permission for the independent researcher to approach the organisation.

At this stage, one organisation declined to take part in the research, while another four failed to reply. Extensive follow-up calls eventually led to three of the latter agreeing to co-operate (the remaining organisation failed to respond at all).

A further two organisations were approached but, within the life of the project, it was only possible to make contact with one, leaving a total of eight organisations included in the research.

Each participating organisation was provided with an information pack on the research. This included separate leaflets for staff and for tenants explaining the research and seeking people who were happy to be interviewed. For tenants, these leaflets were written in a straightforward language and included a photograph of the researcher and various symbols.

At all stages the involvement of individuals was entirely voluntary. For example, the leaflets for the tenants stressed that if they did not want to take part, they simply had to tell support staff they were not interested and they would not be contacted; effectively, there was a process of interested tenants opting in, rather than the onus being on them to opt out.

The approach to staff was rather more direct, although it was made clear that they, too, could choose not to be involved. They were, however, also asked to support the participation of tenants by making sure the tenants got leaflets, explaining them if required, and by passing on the names and details of tenants who were happy to be interviewed.

This rather formal process was devised to ensure that tenants were able to give informed consent to taking part before having any direct contact with an outsider. However, there were still situations where the tenants denied having seen the leaflet at the time of the interview.

The interview schedule for staff was semi-structured, and designed to explore both the issues raised by the user-consultants, and to follow up the findings of the TPAS (Wales) project (Keeble, 1996). These were carried out on a one-to-one basis (occasionally with two members of staff), usually with house managers.

It had been the intention to try to establish a 'management view' as distinct from a front-line staff perspective. In practice, many of the organisations simply nominated the manager of a specific house to speak for them, so the two groups have been merged and are simply referred to as professionals.

In the context of a service for women and children escaping violence (which had a no-men policy) all contact with the research project was with Jenny Hindmoor, then working for the NHHT as a tenant participation officer. Otherwise all the interviews were carried out by the author.

The interviews and group discussions with tenants were designed to be as informal and unintimidating as possible. Tenants would choose when and where to be interviewed, as well as whether it was to be on a one-to-one basis or as a group. In practice, most tenants opted to see the researcher in their house, although one or two did prefer the local pub. Most interviews were carried out without staff being present.

A broad topic list was used to guide the discussion, which was otherwise allowed to reflect the concerns of the tenants as much as possible. Topics included:

- What is it like to live in your house?

- How much control do you have over your life?

- Who decides what happens in your house?

- What happens when something goes wrong, that you do not like?

- Do you have a say in how [the support organisation] works?

- Do you have any contact with the Notting Hill Housing Trust?

- Do you go to any outside groups?

- If you were in charge, what would you change?

Within each topic area, the researcher had prepared a number of supplementary questions designed to open out the discussion.